ANGRY
ALL THE TIME
An Emergency Guide to Anger Control

RON POTTER-EFRON, M.S.W.

NEW HARBINGER PUBLICATIONS, INC.

Publisher's Note

This publication is designed to provide accurate and authoritative information in regard to the subject matter covered. It is sold with the understanding that the publisher is not engaged in rendering psychological, financial, legal, or other professional services. If expert assistance or counseling is needed, the services of a competent professional should be sought.

Angry All The Time
Copyright © 1994 by New Harbinger Publications, Inc.
5674 Shattuck Avenue
Oakland, CA 94609

Cover Digistration ™ and design by SHELBY DESIGNS & ILLUSTRATES
Cover photo by Daniel N. David

Distributed in the U.S.A. by Publishers Group West; in Canada by Raincoast Books; in Great Britain by Airlift Book Company, Ltd.; in South Africa by Real Books, Ltd.; in Australia by Boobook; and in New Zealand by Tandem Press.

Library of Congress Catalog Card Number: 94-067046

ISBN 1-879237-97-0 Paperback

99   98   97

15   14   13   12   11   10   9   8   7

Contents

Introduction

This is not a nice book. It's not supposed to make you feel better. In fact, after you read it you might feel worse for a while—until you start doing things a whole lot smarter.

Face it. If you're reading this book, you probably have a serious problem with anger or violence or both. You get angry over ridiculous things. You say and do stuff you later regret, and then you do the same crap all over again. You've lost friends, lovers, jobs, and maybe your freedom because you can't control your temper. If you haven't lost much yet, you will soon, unless you learn how to do things differently.

You could be a partner of an angry person. He or she is making your life miserable. You've tried everything you can think of to keep things calm, but nothing works. You don't know what to do anymore. You don't want to leave, but you can't live this way.

You could be both. Lots of really angry people live with equally furious partners. Angry people attract other angry people.

I'm not talking about people who get a little too angry once in a while. Hell, no. They're amateurs. They don't need to read this book. Point them to a nice book on assertiveness. They don't know anything about real anger, do they?

But I'll bet you do. You know how to get really mad. You've been so full of rage you couldn't see straight. You've felt like breaking every bone in somebody's body. You've watched yourself losing control. You've *wanted* to lose control so you could smash people and objects. You've thrown stuff and destroyed lots of things with your rage, including relationships. You've hurt people's feelings a lot. But so what. They deserved it, didn't they? You insult your partner, criticize your kids, piss off your friends. And you never, never say you're sorry or admit fault. You blame and shame. You never explain.

You are habitually angry. You get mad so often you've forgotten what it's like not to be angry. Anger is your best friend; maybe your only friend. It's become just about the only feeling you have. Good-bye happiness. So long joy. Forget sadness and fear. What's love got to do with it, anyhow? Anger, anger, and more anger, that's what life is all about nowadays. You're angry all the time.

You're like an oven set on broil or a flamethrower that never runs out of fuel. Yet you wonder why nobody seems to want to get close, don't you.

Resentments and hate, you're good at those too. Let someone mention your "ex" and you start screaming. Your parents can go straight to the devil after what they did to you. You won't even talk to them anymore. You've got more enemies than most people have shirts. Your specialty in school was hate, and you were a straight A student.

This is not an AA book, but the first step in The Twelve Steps of Alcoholics Anonymous sure applies to you. Just change the word *alcohol* to *anger*, and your version might go like this:

> *We are powerless over anger and our lives have become unmanageable.*

Your anger has taken over your whole life. It's got you. You may not want to admit it, but it's got you.*

---

* My original title for this book was *Rageaholic*. Those of you with severe anger problems may choose to call yourself rageaholics. If so, use that label to help you make a commitment to change.

If you don't believe me, try going a week without getting pissed off even once. When that fails, try going twenty-four hours. I'm not talking about wanting to wring somebody's neck and making yourself stop. That's like drinking vodka in the bathroom when nobody's looking. I mean honestly not getting mad about anything. Keeping cool. Chilling out. Good luck, friend. You'll need it.

Angry people come in two genders: male and female. Some are violent. They hurt anybody they can, which usually means people who are smaller than they are. Dad hits Mom. Mom beats the kids. The kids beat smaller kids. The smallest kid kicks the dog.

Some angry people use their mouths like fists. They beat up people with words—mean words like *whore* and *asshole* and other phrases I won't repeat here. They've forgotten how to say anything decent, like "thanks" or "I love you" or "please."

Many angry people are both: they are violent and they attack with their words.

Normal Anger vs. Problem Anger

Everybody gets angry once in a while, but most people know how to deal with their anger. Their anger tells them something is wrong. Then they figure out what's bothering them. They do something to change the bad situation. They check to find out how well their action worked. If what they did or said didn't work, they think about it some more and try something else. If the action worked, they let go of their anger so they can get on with their life.

Here's how the normal chain works. My anger:

- tells me I have a problem

- that I need to think about

- and then say or do something

- and then check out the results

- and then change what I do (if the first thing failed)

- or let go of my anger (if it worked)

Enter the angry person, who does things differently. Here's how. My anger:

- tells me *everything* is a problem
- that I constantly think about
- then I come on *too strong* with what I say and do
- then I *ignore* the bad results
- so I *fail to change* my actions
- and then I *won't let go* of my anger

Familiar? Let's look at the angry person's responses a little closer.

Everything Is a Problem To Get Angry About

Most overly angry people are also overly sensitive. They are too easily hurt, thin-skinned, quick to feel insulted. One result is that they get angry all the time over stuff other people would ignore.

We all get dozens of *anger invitations* every day. An anger invitation is anything that we could use as an excuse to get mad. For instance:

- The driver who cuts in front of you
- The too hot coffee or too cold soda pop
- Your partner saying, "No thanks, dear, not tonight"
- A child who keeps playing when it's supper time
- The lawn that keeps growing
- Someone at work who leaves early and often
- Your partner saying, "Yes, dear, tonight" (just when you were sure you'd be turned down and made other plans)
- Just about everything else people say and do

Other people learn early in life to say "no, thanks" to most anger invitations. Why? Because anger is a lot of work. It tires you out. Besides, if you get mad at everything, that's all you'll feel. There won't be room for anything else.

Habitually angry people say "yes, certainly" to way too many anger invitations. They've never met an anger invitation they didn't like.

The grass keeps growing, does it. It can go to hell and take that damn lawn mower with it. Your partner turns you down. Good! That gives you a chance to complain for hours. Shake your fist at that driver! Throw the soda pop on the floor! Shout at the kids. Tell off that guy at work once and for all! Accuse your partner of being an animal for wanting sex so often!

What's that line from the song? Oh, yeah: "Everything's coming up anger for me and for you." Well, OK, the song says roses, not anger. But we're talking about a thorny problem here. Besides, what right do you have to correct me? I'm writing this book. You're making me mad. You're . . . Oops, I did it again. I got mad over nothing. Sorry.

Constantly Thinking About What Makes You Angry

> I'm so mad at her. She treated me like dirt. I lie in bed for hours thinking of what she did. I wake up in the middle of the night with my teeth clenched. My friends are sick of hearing about it. My parents won't even listen anymore.

Obsession. To think and think and think about something, that's called obsession. Angry people become obsessed with what they're upset about. They think about the harm that's been done, how troubled they are about it, how they can get back at the person who hurt them, and on, and on.

The more you think about what makes you angry, the angrier you get.

It's that simple. You can spend hours dwelling on your anger. But you'll only end up more upset. Anger leads to more anger. Hey, who eats the most ice cream? The people who think about eating ice cream the most, of course. So who do you think "eats" the most anger?

Coming on Too Strong

If only all that thinking led to smart actions. But it doesn't. Instead, the too angry person often says and does things he or she regrets later. Why? Because by now they're convinced that what the other person did is terrible, horrible, awful.

To find out just how terrible something is, I ask the man or woman in my office to use a ten-point scale. Just a tiny bit bad is a one, five is pretty bad, ten is absolutely awful.

"How about that crazy driver?"

"Seven."

"The children not coming in for supper right when you call?"

"Nine."

"Turned down for sex?"

"Eleven."

"Eleven on a ten-point scale?"

"I said 'eleven' and that's what I meant. That's horrible. I can't stand it. I hate it. How can he do that to me? It makes me so mad!"

See what I mean? They get so upset they can't think very well. So when they decide to do something they come on too strong.

The kids get in ten minutes late. Other parents would be a little annoyed. They'd say a word or two. Then everybody would eat in peace. Not the rageaholic. "How dare you come in late! Who do you think you are? Are you trying to question my authority? Well, I won't stand for it. You can make your own meals from now on."

On and on it goes, all through supper. Another meal ruined. Maybe next time the kids won't come in at all.

No sex? "Turn me down again, huh! Well, that's the last time. I'm outta here. That'll make you pay."

First, angry people accept too many anger invitations. Then they get way too bothered about them. Then they say and do foolish things that only make the situation worse. What else could you do to mess things up?

Plenty! Read on.

Ignoring Bad Results

"Hey, that was great. Keep doing it."

"No, that's not working. Try something else."

Feedback. Ed Koch, the ex-mayor of New York City, went around every day asking New Yorkers one question: "How am I doing?" He lasted several terms, partly because he listened to their answers.

Angry people get a lot of negative feedback from partners, families, employers, and friends. They get lots of messages telling them to relax, to quit being so angry. They ignore these messages.

> What do you mean, relax! How can I when she did that to me? Don't tell me to ease up, buddy. I have a right to be angry!

In fact, they tell themselves they are doing just fine. "It's those imbeciles out there who have a problem with my anger, not me. I wanna be mad right now and nobody can stop me." Right you are. Nobody can stop you but you. And you aren't interested.

I'll be talking soon (in Chapter 3) about the *anger rush.* That's the surge of adrenalin that you get when you're really angry. The rush keeps people angry partly because it feels good. It's a powerful feeling that's hard to give up. That rush also makes it hard to get accurate feedback. The anger feels right. True, others say it's wrong. But it feels right. Better ignore them. Stay angry.

Don't Change a Thing—Even Though It Isn't Working

Ree Lasker, a recovering alcoholic with a wonderful sense of humor, tells a story about a "drunk" and a "normie." Both are sitting in a room with two doors. The normie goes out the first door. Boom! There's a huge guy out there who clobbers him with a baseball bat. He falls back into the room, rests a bit, and goes out the other door, which is unguarded.

Now it's the drunk's turn. He immediately heads out the first door. Boom! He gets smacked. He falls down. He gets up and walks out the same door. Boom! And again. Boom! He stumbles around, stunned, only to head out the same door for the fourth time. This time, no guy with the baseball bat. No boom! So he goes looking for him!

Why do angry people keep going out that same door? Why don't they change? There are at least two reasons.

First, they believe their anger is useful. They aren't hearing the bad news. They don't want to hear it. "Ron, you tell me my anger's a problem. But when I get really mad I get what I want. You're all wrong." Oh yeah? Aren't you forgetting the bad results? The endless arguments. The people who still won't talk with you. The troubles at work. *Your anger is doing much more harm than good.* Admit it.

Second, angry people stay mad because they don't know what else to do. They've been angry so long, that's all they're good at. They have become anger specialists. They're awfully good at what they do. But start talking about other feelings and they get uncomfortable.

People who keep doing the same thing usually get the same results. You will too.

Don't Let Go of Your Anger

Some people cling to their anger as if it were a life raft on a raging sea. They have a motto: never forgive and never forget.

Sure, Billy apologized for standing you up at lunch. But let's not accept that apology. Stay mad. That will show him.

Some angry people don't know what to do when they're not angry. That's one reason they stay so angry. Anger is their "lifestyle." They don't have another.

Besides, they've got to get ready for the next anger invitation. They can't let their guard down. You never know when something might happen they can get mad about. This way angry people stay ready for trouble. They never quite relax. They're always a little angry, just waiting for the next round.

Put all these habits together and you have somebody in big trouble. The habitually angry person gets mad too easily, stays mad too long, and uses that anger poorly.

Why? Why would anyone want to become so angry? That's like asking why someone would want to become an alcoholic. You don't choose it. You become it. But this is important: *You, and only you, can do something to quit being so angry.* Not your lover. Not your friends. Not your probation officer, teacher, mother or father, or the guy sitting next to you on the bus. You.

The Rest of the Book

Well, then, what exactly do you have to do to quit being so angry? For starters, read this book. It's divided into two parts, understanding the problem and taking action, and eleven chapters.

Chapter 1: My Life Is a Mess Because of My Anger. Frankly, if you're life was great, you wouldn't be reading this. Your anger is screwing you up. You're getting in trouble. Your health may be going bad because of your anger. You've been so mean that you don't even like yourself anymore. It's time to get honest with yourself before your life gets worse.

Chapter 2: Why? Why? Why? Why Did I Become So Angry? Why did this happen? What's made me so angry? Was it the family I grew up in? Bad luck? Is there something wrong with my mind? This chapter sorts through some of the ways people learn to be angry all the time. But don't look for excuses here, just explanations. No matter how crummy a life you've had, there is no excuse for continuing to make a royal mess out of the present.

Chapter 3: Why Can't I Stop? The Six Main Reasons People Stay Angry. One or more of these six things keeps you angry: power and control, giving away responsibility, poor communication skills, the anger rush, a defense against feelings and closeness, habit.

Chapter 4: The Anger and Violence Ladder. There are eight steps on this ladder. The lowest one is for sneaky anger—things like forgetting on purpose. The top rung is blind rage, where the goal is to destroy whatever gets in your way.

Chapter 5: Fish or Cut Bait—It's Time To Make a Promise. Shit or get off the pot. Here's your chance to make a commitment to changing your life. Not a one-day promise. Not an "I'll try, but . . . " guarantee of failure. Either you plan to take steps to quit being a rageaholic, or you're wasting your time.

Chapter 6: Climbing Down the Ladder, Part 1—No More Violence or Threats. Pretty obvious, isn't it? Or is it? It takes a lot of guts to give up bullying tactics. Do you have the courage to talk about stuff instead of throwing a tantrum?

Chapter 7: Climbing Down the Ladder, Part 2—Keep That Foul Mouth Shut Until You Learn To Talk Right. It's so easy to bad-mouth people. But I'll help you learn better ways to talk, if you're ready to use them. It's called respectful communication. Give it to others and you might even get some back.

Chapter 8: Believe It or Not, They're Not Out To Get You. Paranoia, anyone? Let's look at the crazy thoughts angry people have that make them create enemies. No, your partner doesn't hate you. If he or she did, they'd be gone by now. It's time to get your thoughts clear.

Chapter 9: Saying Good-bye to Old Resentments. I know, they're old friends. But do you really want to hang on to ancient hatreds, when all they do is make you sick inside? Are you ever going to be ready to get on with your life?

Chapter 10: I Need Help, Too—A Chapter for Partners of Angry People. Am I crazy for loving him? What do I do when she goes nuts? Should I stay or get the hell out? Am I getting to be way too angry myself?

If you're going to stick around, you need a survival plan. If you decide to leave, don't mess it up with useless guilt feelings.

Chapter 11: Where Do I Go from Here? Asking for what you want is a skill. To learn it, you must be willing to quit trying to manipulate, con, or threaten others. Fair fighting is possible, but not until you quit raging.

To repeat, my goal is not to help you feel good. Not now. You need to feel lousy for a while. You're a habitually angry person, a member of one of the least happy groups known to humankind. You've earned every bit of your misery. Now how about doing something about it so the rest of your life isn't as bad as it's been up till now?

PART I

Understanding

1

My Life Is a Mess
Because of My Anger

Anger is a strong feeling. It can get you into a lot of trouble. Want to find out how much trouble you have with anger? Of course not! It's easier to *deny* the problem. "Who, me angry? They must be thinking of somebody else. I never get mad." Or to *minimize*: "Well, maybe I have a little anger problem, but it really isn't that bad." Or to *blame* others: "Well, sure I get steamed a lot, but it's all his (her) fault."

Let's cut through the crap right now. You're no innocent victim. You're not the nicest person walking around.

Be honest. No more bullshit. Quit lying to yourself. You are an angry person. A very angry person. A rageaholic.

Need proof? Read on. You're going to provide it, if you're honest.

What a Mess—The Results of
Long-term Anger

Turn the page to see a large circle cut into eight pieces. That circle is like a pie, and each piece is a slice of your life. It's your own personal *anger pie*. Each slice is one major area of your life that you have damaged because of your anger.

Take a look at the names of the slices.

- Health
- Family
- Work and school
- Money
- Friends
- The law
- Mood and personality
- Values and spirit

I'm going to tell you about some of the most common problems angry people run into in each of these areas. Meanwhile, you write down the ones that you've encountered. There may be others not on my list. Put them on too.

Health

> *Here lies Dirty Dan*
> *He was an angry man*
> *Always crabby, always mad*
> *He died young, and we're glad*

Unless you do something about your anger soon, that's what your tombstone may look like.

Charles Spielberger is a psychologist who has studied anger. He, and many others, discovered that anger is a health hazard. He isn't talking about just getting mad for a few minutes once in a while—that's normal. He's talking about staying angry for long periods of time or getting furious a lot.

Too much anger can kill you. How? Anger triggers the "fight or flight" response—the surge of adrenalin. Strong anger is an emergency reaction. It is as if your body is saying, "Danger, danger, do something now, be alert." Your blood pressure rises and stays high long after the danger is over. As a result angry people suffer heart attacks and strokes. The angrier you get, and stay, the more likely you are to die young. If you don't believe me, look in the mirror the next time you get

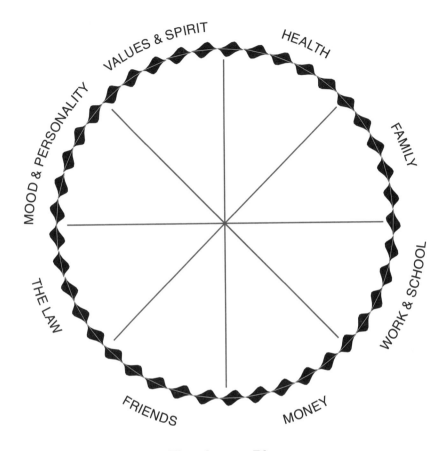

The Anger Pie

pissed. The red face. The clenched fists. You're like a pressure cooker getting ready to explode. Long-term anger can take years off your life.

But that's not the only health risk. What about the time you got so mad you punched your fist through the window and needed twenty stitches to close the wound, or the time you broke bones hitting the wall.

If you're a fighter, how many times have you been clobbered? Knocked out? Hospitalized? Maybe you beat them up, too, but all those fights wouldn't happen if you didn't have such a short fuse.

An angry person behind the wheel of a car is an accident waiting to happen. Or do you always spin out of the driveway and hit sixty miles per hour in ten seconds?

Angry people don't just get mad at others. They sometimes hate themselves, too. That's when they do things like smacking themselves on the head ("I'm so stupid, stupid, stupid") or cutting or burning.

And then there are the blackouts caused by rage. These aren't drinking blackouts, although drinking makes them more common. These are times you get so angry that you almost lose consciousness. You don't pass out, though. You do all kinds of dangerous things, like yell and scream, attack the whole gang at the bar, go berserk. These blackouts are a sign that your anger is out of control.

Is this fun? No! Then do something before you die at age fifty from an aneurysm directly related to a lifetime of anger.

Turn back to the anger pie on page 17 and put in the health problems that are related to your anger.

Family

Go back and read the epitaph again. Why do you think the last line says "He died young, and we're glad"? Because living with an angry person is a bad trip, that's why.

It's not that your partner or kids quit loving you, although they might. Who could blame them for not loving someone who complains, nags, bullies, and tries to control all the time? But even if they still love you, what good does it do? Ever try to say nice things to somebody screaming her head off? It doesn't work and you feel crummy.

After a while your loved ones just stay away.

I've had moms and dads tell me how much they wish their kids would talk with them, or stay home more, or just be there. Then I speak with the kids. They tell me they keep away because Mom or Dad is always angry. Dad gets in a rage over little things that hardly matter. Mom hasn't said anything nice in weeks.

Does your family avoid you because of your anger? Do they walk on tiptoes around you? (If you want them to be afraid of you, read Chapter 3 very carefully.)

Have you lost a partner because of your anger, or even partly because of your anger? Is it happening again, right now?

Do you and your partner fight a lot? By a lot I mean at least one serious "I'm really mad at you now" fight every day or two or *any fight that is violent.* Have you become The Battling Couple or The Fighting Family—the kind that nobody wants to be around anymore because you spoil everybody's fun?

Remember Jackie Gleason in "The Honeymooners"? Ralph and Alice fought every night. But they always made up by the end of the show. In real life angry couples don't do that. They stay angry for days or weeks at a time. Hot anger. Cold anger. Nasty stuff.

Here is an important question: Who in your family is concerned about your anger? If even one person is worried, you probably have an anger problem. If more than one, it's almost certain. Go talk to them now. Find out what they know about your anger. Be sure to take the wax out of your ears. Listen. Don't lecture. Don't defend. Don't deny. Just listen as hard as you can.

Family problems often show up around holidays and special times. How do you get through Christmas, or Thanksgiving, or even Sunday night supper? Are you usually annoyed, upset, bothered, bugged? Rageaholics usually have a lousy time. They often make sure others do too.

Are you physically abusing loved ones? If you are hitting, shoving, pinching, or keeping people from leaving when they want, you have a serious problem.

Then there's emotional abuse. If you scream or yell, insult your loved ones, shame them and blame them, you have a serious anger problem.

And what about the family you grew up in? Are you feuding with some of them? Do your resentments keep you away?

Family is supposed to be about love, not hate. Long-term anger destroys families. Don't let it destroy yours.

Turn back to the anger pie on page 17 and put in the family problems that are related to your anger.

Work and School

Warnings. Disciplinary actions. Suspensions. Lost promotions. Firings.

An employer called me recently:

> Ron, I've got a great worker. I'd like to make her an office manager. But I'm not sure I can even keep her. She just gets so angry. One minute she's fine. The next she's yelling her head off at someone. She's unpredictable. Can you help her learn to control her temper?

Well, yes, I can. The first step, though, is for this woman to realize she's got a big anger problem.

When we talked, she began by blaming her boss, and the work crew, and the gossip. Then she got honest with herself. This was the third job she was ruining with her anger. She'd been fired once and dead-ended another time. She was educated. She was intelligent. And she was a rageaholic at work.

Constant fighting with people in authority is one type of work problem. Regular battles with equals is another. Getting furious with the people you are boss of is a third.

No wonder they don't want you to join them for lunch. Would you?

Changing jobs a lot because of anger is called *geographical escape*. But you take your anger with you to the next job. Same behavior, same results.

School is similar to work. Add a touch of teenage defiance ("I'm my own boss and nobody better tell me what to do"). Subtract a little adult wisdom and maturity. You end up with a rebel and a young rager learning to get mad at the world.

Again, turn back to the anger pie and put in the work and school problems that are related to your anger.

Money

Anger is an expensive habit. First comes replacing all the things you destroy: telephones, glass, dishes, dinners, your kids' toys, the television set you tossed through the window, automobiles—yours and others'—trees you cut down when you got pissed. Anything and everything. It feels good for a couple of seconds, doesn't it? And then it doesn't feel so great.

Think of the medical costs for accidents while you were angry. Visits to the emergency room—maybe for you, maybe for someone you hurt. We're talking big bucks here, but some of the costs can never be repaid.

How about legal fines? Drunk and disorderly. Disturbing the peace.

> Mr. Jones, that will cost you $350 plus court costs. Next case, please. Oh, it's you again, Mr. Jones. Well, this time it will cost you $500 plus court costs.

Now here's the real messy part. How about that terrible divorce, when you got so angry at your wife. You swore you would get the kids—just to hurt her—even if it cost your life savings. Well, you were half right. You spent all your savings. Did you really believe the children's lawyer would support your case after you lost your temper and called her a feminist bitch?

That child support is expensive, too.

Turn back to the anger pie and put in the money problems that are related to your anger.

Friends

> He used to be my one best friend
> Until he made me mad
> I'm way too proud to make amends
> But man I feel so sad

We all need friends. But angry people ruin their friendships. Sooner or later they pick a fight. And then another fight. And a third. Your friend tries to patch things up, of course. But if you're always angry you don't really want to end the arguing. Fighting is what you do best. It's what you're used to. Better to lose that friend than to quit being angry.

The arguments may become violent. Friends beat up friends, don't they?

Many angry people can count their friends on their thumbs. One, maybe two. Maybe none left. The results: isolation and loneliness. You're angry about being so alone. But your anger is a big reason for it. Quit being so angry, and you might get back some of those old friends, and make a few new ones.

There's one other pattern. Maybe all your friends these days are as angry as you. That's great. Misery loves company. Stick with the losers and you'll be one yourself.

Turn back to the anger pie and put in the friendship problems that are related to your anger.

The Law

I once lived in a house where the police cruised by every fifteen minutes. Just checking. Nice guys, once you got to know them. Don't know why they were so worried about us. It couldn't have had anything to do with our anger, I'm sure.

Exactly how well do you want to get to know your local constables? Are you already on a first name basis? If not, just stay angry and you soon will be.

I've already mentioned drunk and disorderly and disturbing the peace. But what about those house calls for domestic problems? Perhaps nobody was arrested, but still they came as a result of your inability to control your anger.

Restraining orders are more than a little annoying. Yet, to the angry person, it's always their fault, not mine. I'm a peace-loving fellow (or gal), I don't make trouble. It's all a misunderstanding. They're out to get me.

Violently angry people get ordered to programs for batterers and child abusers. In fact, that may be why you're reading this page right now. It's just one more sign that you are in big trouble with your anger.

Turn back to the anger pie and put in legal problems that are related to your anger.

Mood and Personality

Remember Dr. Jekyll, that gentle scientist, and the evil Mr. Hyde, the man he became when he drank a nasty potion? You may be the nicest man or woman in the whole world when you're not angry. But look what happens when you get mad. The beast comes out. You go out of control.

Loss of control increases the longer you stay angry. The anger takes over. You change. You become more suspicious, paranoid, nastier—even when you think you're not angry.

Angry people gradually build up a tolerance for their own anger. That means they get used to their anger. And that means they need to get more and more angry just to feel the feeling. They train themselves to become angrier human beings. And sometimes they train their whole families. "Oh, that's just dad blowing off steam again," they say. "We don't take him seriously anymore until he throws things around." The madder you get now, the angrier you'll be in a few years.

Turn back to the anger pie and put in the mood and personality changes that are related to your anger.

Values and Spirit

Guilt and shame. They come when you've hurt people with your anger—people you never wanted to harm—again.

> How could I do that to them? Why did I say such terrible things? I know they're not true, but I was so angry. I just wanted to hurt them. I did. And now I feel awful. What kind of a person would keep getting so angry? There's something wrong with me!

This guilt and shame comes too late. It's like closing the barn door after the horse got out. Sure, you feel bad. But you'll keep getting angry unless you make some real changes in your life. The guilt and shame have to come *before* you blow your stack, not after. Then you can take a time-out, or sit down and shut up, or compromise, or do a dozen other things so that you can look yourself in the mirror afterwards.

Make a list of your values: honesty, fairness, responsibility to your family, for example. Include whatever is on your personal list of important things to live by. Now ask yourself how well you live up to those values when you're storming around having a fit. Chances are you forget about honesty, and fairness, and responsibility to your family, and your other values. All you want to do is win. And make them pay. And hurt them.

Hate fits in here. Hate keeps you trapped. Hate damages the human spirit. It keeps you from growing. It's a weed in the garden of life. it spreads quickly. Sometimes it destroys all the flowers, all the joy.

Some habitually angry people are furious with God. "Well, God, what have you done for me lately?" they ask, still fuming because He never gave them the breaks they think they deserve. They shake their fists at the sky.

Finally, angry people become *mean-spirited*. Something crumbles deep inside. They sense that something awful has happened to them. Peace is gone. Serenity is a dim memory. Happiness seems impossible, and it is—until you accept reality.

Turn back to the anger pie and put in the problems you're having with values and spirit because of your anger.

Summary

Take a good look now at your anger pie. You have an anger problem if any slice of that pie is filled up with the results of your anger. *Negative consequences* (that's the technical name for all the bad stuff that results from your anger) are the final products of years or perhaps a lifetime of anger.

The more slices with anger problems, the worse that pie will taste. If most or all of the slices are filled with anger, your whole life is going to be bitter-tasting.

Do you have a serious anger problem? You bet, if that pie is full from your anger.

2

Why? Why? Why? Why Did I Become So Angry?

OK, now you're facing reality. You are in big trouble. But how did this happen? Were you born angry? Did it begin in childhood? As a teenager? After you became an adult? Do you have a serious mental problem, physical illness, or alcohol/drug problem?

We're looking for explanations here, not excuses. *You and only you are responsible for your anger.* But it might help you to make changes if you know how you got so angry.

Each of us has his or her story. Here's mine. When I was nine years old my mother died. My father never recovered from that blow. He became depressed, and then he began dying from diabetes. He lost his sense of humor. He got irritable and sarcastic. He was angry a lot, and almost never happy. He didn't hit us, but the whole family followed his lead. We all got angry, mean, sarcastic, and grumpy. Life wasn't fun anymore. We argued with each other much of the time. Anger was the main emotion in our home for a decade.

I got lucky. After my Dad died I was shown how to love, first by kind relatives and then by Pat, my wife to be. It took years to let go of most of the anger. I still have to be careful. It's easy to fall back into the old crap. I just know I don't ever

want to live like that again. It's up to me now to make sure
I don't.

What's your story?

Angry People Come from Angry Families

The single most common cause of severe anger is an angry home.
Kids learn how angry they should be from their parents. They
learn when to get angry. And how. And how much. It's called
modeling.

Severely angry families do things differently than normal
ones. They have three destructive habits:

- They think a lot of anger is normal and expected.
- Nobody listens until you get angry.
- They try to solve their problems with anger.

Let's look at these habits one at a time.

In Angry Families a Lot of Anger Is Normal and Expected

Anger has one great value. *Anger is a sign that something
is wrong.* But in some families anger is like a broken warning
signal at a railroad crossing. It keeps flashing and buzzing
when there are no trains coming.

People in these families get mad all the time. There may
be good reasons to get angry. If not, though, they make them
up.

Everybody in these families is expected to be angry. Someone is almost always angry at someone else. There is at least
a feud a day. Or perhaps practically everyone is mad at
everyone else.

It's like a free-for-all wrestling match, a soap opera, a
strange baseball game. "Hey, get your scorecard here! Find
out who hates who today." Never a dull moment in these
families.

Have you ever been invited to dinner with an angry
family? Maybe you didn't know they were so troubled until

you rang the doorbell. The door opens to the sounds of fighting. Dad is yelling at the kids. Mom is screaming at Dad. Little Jackie is "just teasing" her smaller brother to tears. Nobody listens.

They don't calm down just because you're there. Oh, maybe a little, but the fighting keeps on. Tension fills the air during silences. There are threats, insults, put-downs for no reason, and senseless bickering.

The worst part is all that fighting seems *normal* to them. Normal. Routine. Everyday behavior. That means they fight like that all the time. They weren't putting on a show to impress you. They really are an angry family.

Think of those kids. What will all that fighting do to them? What will they learn? To be angry all the time when they grow up. (Some adults from angry families swear they'll never be like that, they'll never get angry. Even so, they often blow up over nothing because they were trained that way.)

In Angry Families Nobody Listens Until You Get Angry

Sixteen-year-old Missy argues with her mother. They trade insults. They threaten each other. Missy bangs the table. Her mom screams at her to shut up.

No big deal, though. They do this a lot, since anger is normal.

But then Mom picks up the sugar bowl and hurls it right at Missy's head, missing her by inches.

"Hey, why'd you do that?" Missy shouts.

"Because," Mom shouts back, "that's the only way to make you listen to me."

That's how to get someone's attention, by getting more and more angry.

First I only had to talk loud. But that got old. So
then I yelled. But then they just laughed. Now I
have to act a little crazy. They completely ignore me
if I don't. I guess when that quits working I'll have
to smack someone.

Not only you but everybody in the family has to get angrier to be heard. You've trained each other to listen only to anger.

Adults have asked me why others think they're so angry. Here's why. They're too loud. They think the only way to talk is to shout. They're way too pushy. The sad part is, they are only doing what they learned at home.

Were you raised in this kind of family? Is that where you began to be a rageaholic?

Angry Families Try To Solve Problems with Anger

Maybe you grew up in a family that tried to handle its troubles with anger.

Joe skipped school today? OK, one three-hour lecture coming up.

Dad looked too long at that pretty brunet, did he? "Where's the shotgun? I'll kill that no-good bastard."

Jill ate two pieces of pie? "That's it, she's gonna get a piece of my mind next!"

Your teenager lied to you. Ground her forever!

"How could you do this to me!"

"I'm so mad at you I'll never forgive you."

"You made me angry. Now you're gonna pay."

Anger is badly misused in these families. People try to solve their problems by getting mad. That won't work. It's like trying to turn a screw with a hammer. *Anger is a signal, not a solution.* Remember that. You can't solve your problems with anger. The anger tells you there's a problem. That's all. The problem may be inside you (you woke up with a sinus headache). It may be outside you (the kids broke a window playing ball). But just getting angry won't solve either problem. The anger tells you to do something smart. It's not a license to lose control. Anger itself doesn't solve problems. It creates them.

To repeat: *Angry people come from angry families.* But did you notice the examples I gave were about the present, not the past. That's because *angry people often live in angry families now.*

Did you grow up in an angry family? How often were your parents angry? How did they handle their anger? Did you learn from them to be angry too soon, too hard, too long?

Have you started a new angry family? Are you passing along the habit of rage to another generation?

Let's put a stop to it now. You don't need to do to your kids what was done to you.

More Ways To Become Too Angry

It sure helps to grow up in an angry family. But there are many other ways to become habitually angry.

Physical or Sexual Abuse

Angry people are often the victims of long-term physical abuse. They survived, but they were badly damaged. They can't put the abuse behind them. Instead, they seem to remember every blow. Each humiliation. All those moments of sheer terror. They get angry every time they remember. They become enraged.

They dream about revenge. "Oh, if I could get my hands on that SOB now, I'd . . ."

Sometimes they got a little revenge, but even then it wasn't enough.

> Ron, my father hit me every day. Then I got strong. One day he started to beat my mother. I went nuts. I threw him up against the wall. I wanted to kill him, but I didn't. I ran out of the house. But you know what? He never laid a hand on me or her again! My only regret is I didn't kill him when I had the chance.

Happy ending? No way. He's in my office because he's been striking his girlfriend. He hates himself for doing it, but he can't stop. He's terrified of having children. He's afraid he'll hurt them. And he will if he doesn't change.

Unfortunately, victims of physical abuse often grow up to be abusers. They say to themselves, "Hey, it's my turn now, damn it. I got hit when I was small. Now I'm big. I can hurt others like they hurt me."

Or they may just become bitter, angry, resentful.

Perhaps you are a survivor of sexual abuse. You held down your rage for years. Then it blasted through. Now you hate. You don't know what to do with that hate. It's destroying your life. You're pushing people away as if they had some disgusting disease. You push away everyone who reminds you of the abuse—men with mustaches, older men, women with loud voices, men and women. You too want revenge, but your anger is mixed with fear. You don't know whether to fight or run away. Sometimes you do both.

You've got to deal with your past if your anger is due partly to physical or sexual abuse. And don't try to do it alone. There are people out there who can assist you. Abuse isn't a secret anymore. You don't have to be ashamed. Getting help with the abuse will also help with the anger.

Shame

Shame means feeling bad about ourselves—our whole selves—not just what we do, but who we are. When I feel ashamed it's as if there's something very bad about me that won't go away.

Shamed persons tell themselves five messages:

- I'm no good.
- I'm not good enough.
- I'm not loved or lovable.
- I don't belong.
- I shouldn't even be alive.

Pat Potter-Efron and I have written a lot about shame (see *Letting Go of Shame**). I suggest you read it if you feel bad about yourself or if you say these things to yourself frequently.

---

* *Letting Go of Shame,* by Pat and Ron Potter-Efron, published in 1989 by Hazelden/Harper, Center City, MN.

Shame connects in three main ways to anger. First, some people feel shame whenever they get angry. These people usually avoid their anger, even when they have plenty of reason to get mad, because it feels so awful. They become *anger avoiders.*

Second, deeply shamed people (those who feel way too much shame) often lead bitter, frustrated lives. They are constantly angry at themselves. Nothing they do is ever good enough. They are full of self-hatred.

Third, shamed persons are likely to strike out at others a lot. Because I am full of shame, practically anything you say or do touches it. For example, you try to tell me nicely I made a spelling error. But I take it personally. How dare you criticize me! You must think I'm stupid, don't you? Well, I'll show you who's the real dummy. You're the idiot, not me. And on and on I go. I thought you were deliberately shaming me, so I shamed you right back.

Shame and anger make a nasty combination. It's called rage.

You may need professional help if you rage a lot because of shame. You'll need to learn to like and respect yourself. It's a long road, but worth traveling.

Alcohol

Hey, leave my booze out of this. Sure I get
mad a lot when I drink. But it's none of your
business. I've got an anger problem, not an
alcohol problem.

Well, exc*uuuuu*se me, but that's called denial, the big D, as in death trip.

We can't leave booze out of it, not if you've got an anger problem. We also better take a good look at other drugs.

First off, if you are an alcoholic, you won't get anywhere with your anger until you get help with that problem. You'll spend too much time figuring out reasons to be angry. Then you can use your anger to excuse your drinking.

Hell, I wouldn't have a drinking problem if those
idiots would leave me alone. Morons. I get mad just
thinking about them. Bartender, another beer, quick!

By the way, several studies on anger and alcoholism show
that the two problems are practically twins. Over half the
people being treated for alcoholism also have big-time anger
problems. And even recovering alcoholics have trouble with
anger. That's what a *dry drunk* is all about. A dry drunk stays
off the sauce but ignores other problems, such as out-of-control
anger.

What if you're not an alcoholic? You may still get angrier
when you drink. You may use being loaded as an excuse for
your anger ("Yeah, I was a jerk, but it was the booze. I'm not
that kind of a person").

That's bull. *You are responsible for what you put in your
mouth, nose, or arm—and for everything you say or do with that
stuff inside you.* No exceptions. Alcohol and drugs don't give
us a time-out from reality.

But Ron, you've got it wrong. I drink to mellow out.
That's how I cool off. I'm afraid I could kill someone if I quit drinking.

Yes, some people do use booze or drugs (especially
marijuana) to avoid their anger. It works for a while, sometimes. And then they explode. I call this pattern "stuff and
blow." Stuff the anger down. More. More. Use drugs to help.
Don't ever deal with the real issues. Avoid, avoid, avoid.
Kablooey!

Other Drugs

There are *no* safe mood-altering drugs if you're too angry.
None.

Marijuana. Let's get the myths about of marijuana out
of the way first. It doesn't make everybody mellow. It doesn't
stop anger. Recent studies show that long-term marijuana use
does the opposite. It adds to a person's anger. It's a dangerous
drug, especially if you are even a little paranoid. (*Paranoid*

means you are overly suspicious, distrustful, or think people are out to harm you.) One of the angriest individuals I've ever seen smoked pot daily. He was stoned most of the day. He was angry most of the day. When he stopped smoking marijuana he had a lot less trouble with rage.

Cocaine. You might as well order the license plate "HOS-TILE." One study of a cocaine hot line found that 99 percent of the callers complained of feeling irritable, guarded, and suspicious. Regular cocaine users develop or increase their anger problems.

PCP (Angel Dust). This drug makes people aggressive even if they never were before. It's about as nasty as you get. Don't even think about using PCP if you have an anger problem. Don't even think about thinking about it if you get angry a lot.

Amphetamines (Speed). Go ahead, use speed, if you want to get thrown in the mental wards as a paranoid schizophrenic. Long-term use warps your mind—in the direction of rage.

Sedatives (Downers). Sedatives are closely associated with violence and suicidal behavior. They are a disinhibitor like alcohol.

Anabolic Steroids. People who use these drugs to build up their bodies often get and stay angry. One trouble is that people will tell you that you're different, but you won't believe them. And, man, will that piss you off! Watch out for steroids in prescription medications, like Prednisone.

Hallucinogens (LSD, Mescaline). Like marijuana, avoid hallucinogens if you have any tendency toward paranoia or other mental health problems. Remember that LSD exaggerates everything you think and feel. What will happen if you get angry while tripping?

Opiates (Heroin). You'll probably be too doped up to get angry while high, but how are you going to pay for it? That's where you get into problems with violence.

Physical and Emotional Illness

It's time to get a good physical. Why? Because lots of physical and emotional illnesses can increase anger. Here are a few:

- Chronic pain. A back injury nags and nags. It keeps you from working. It won't go away. You try to stay positive, but . . .

- Brain injuries. From falls, accidents, beatings, or disease, they impair judgment and mix poorly with alcohol.

- Attention deficit disorder, both in children and adults. "Hotheadedness" is one of the characteristics for adults.

- PMS (premenstrual syndrome). Connected with irritability and violence among some women, it makes a bad situation worse for already angry women.

- Depression. Depressed people are often irritable, grouchy, gloomy. The anger may be directed against others, but suicide is another danger.

- PTSD (post-traumatic stress disorder). Some Vietnam war veterans or trauma victims suffer from this. Flashbacks confuse past with present.

This is just a sampler. There are lots of other physical and emotional illnesses that add to anger problems. If you have any medical condition, ask your doctor if it might be adding to your anger. Also ask if the medications you are on could have side effects, such as agitation, that make it worse.

We Live in an Angry World

American society promotes anger in many ways. We are taught to be supercompetitive. Others are rivals who are trying to defeat and destroy us. We are told always to be on guard. Watch out, they're out to get us. Who knows who "they" are, these enemies that circle around us, but they're there. Aren't they?

It seems that only "winners" command respect in a world where it's getting harder and harder just to stay even. It's all too easy to feel like a loser—an angry, defensive loser.

Violence is increasing. More and more prisons are being built, but there are never enough of them to lock away all the dangerous people. Killing has become almost a sport in some areas. To some it's recreation—something to pass the time when you're bored.

Each generation has its wars. We learned to despise the Germans and Japanese, then the communists, then the Iraqis. Who will be next?

We find ways to hate our neighbors, turning them into the forces of evil. Blacks are pitted against whites, straights against gays, pro-lifers against pro-choicers. They're different from us. Good. That's an excuse to use the anger that's been building up inside; a way to deal with frustrations without ever having to look inside.

I'm not saying that American society makes us angry. It doesn't. But it doesn't tell us to stop, either. Macho men and tough women get a lot of encouragement to get mad and to stay mad.

There's a practical point in all of this. *Don't surround your-self with angry people if you want to become less angry.* That's like hoping to cool off by diving into a volcano. Find a few calm and steady persons to hang out with. Maybe you'll learn something from them. At least they won't encourage you to stay angry.

Summary

You don't become angry overnight. Chances are it took time for you to learn how. You may have come from an angry family. If so, you have to quit thinking that a lot of anger is normal. It isn't. You'll need to start listening to others when they aren't mad. And you'll want to start searching for better ways to solve problems, since anger is a good signal of trouble, but a lousy solution.

You'll have to deal with the pain of physical or sexual abuse and separate the past from the present, to give you hope.

Alcohol and drugs have to go. You can't afford to let them affect you when you already have so much trouble with losing control.

You need to get a good physical and mental checkup. Many illnesses add to anger problems.

Watch who you hang out with. Stick with the winners. That means people who have a normal amount of anger. Avoid other habitually angry people. Don't buy into the idea that you are supposed to be angry, no matter who tells you that.

Those are some answers to the question, "Why did I become so angry?" You've used this chapter to help discover how you got into this mess. Remember, though, it's your mess and your job to clean it up.

Let's continue. Next we think about now. What keeps you so angry?

3

Why Can't I Stop?
The Six Main Reasons
People Stay Angry

Why am I still so angry? What keeps me raging?

History is history. It's over. Whatever got you this angry won't change. Better accept that about your life. True acceptance means giving up any last hopes that you can change your past.

The key question is, what keeps you going? Why do you continue to get so angry?

It's back to honesty time. Your anger is doing something for you. It has some uses. If not, you'd let go of it fast. So what keeps you so angry? One or more of these six things:

- Power and control
- Giving away responsibility
- Poor communication skills
- Avoiding other feelings or people
- Habit
- The anger rush

Power and Control

"I want what I want and I want it now!" That's the real reason most people stay angry. Power and control. I can make you do what I want if I get mad enough.

> Who, me? I don't want control. That's not why I get mad. It's them. They're the ones trying to tell me what to do. They're the ones who want power.

Bull. *You* want to be in charge . . . and so do they . . . and so do I. Everybody wants to control others. If we could get away with it, of course, we'd tell everybody else what to do. Dictator For Life.

Power. The ability to make somebody do something. Everybody wants power. You're no different.

Angry people are power trippers. They want control, and the way they get it is to rage. They yell, threaten, call people names, hit. Nasty stuff, but it works. Or at least it used to work.

The trouble is that anger is a crude weapon. Sure, you can control others for a while with your anger, but not for long and not well.

Look. If I hold a gun to your head, you probably will do whatever I demand. But what will happen the moment I turn away or fall asleep? You'll either run or grab the gun and shoot me.

That's the trouble with using anger for control. It's short-term and very expensive. It doesn't last, and it costs you your friends, family, and your own well-being.

Ragers Are Terrorists

You are a terrorist because you are trying to control others with fear. I know, that sounds awful. But it's the truth. Anybody who uses anger and rage to scare others is a terrorist.

Angry people use force to try to make others do things. The anger says, "Do it or else! I'm bigger than you, or louder, or meaner, or angrier. I can make you do what I want. And you better not try to stop me, or I'll get even angrier."

Does this sound childlike? Well, it is. Some angry people haven't completely grown up yet. Like little kids, they throw tantrums when they don't get what they want. They scream. They kick. They hit. They pout. They cry. "I want, I want, I want. Gimme, gimme."

Isn't it time to learn a few better ways to influence people? Instead of yelling, try talking calmly. Try compromising instead of bullying. Listen rather than lecture.

Giving Away Responsibility

It's all their fault, right? Everything would be fine if it weren't for those jerks out there making you mad.

"You make me mad. It's all your fault." That right there is the single excuse I hear the most. It's the rageaholic's theme song. "You make me mad."

Blaming others is how the rageaholic avoids taking responsibility for his or her own choices and actions.

Here's an example. Hedda is a thirty-year-old accountant and homemaker with an eating disorder and a long history of alcoholism (she's sober now, though). She gets furious at least two or three times a day at her husband, her kids, her boss, her friends. What's the problem? Why, every one of those idiots tries to tell her what to do. And they're so ungrateful. And they tell lies. And they're out to get her. And they don't appreciate the wonderful things she does for them. And so on and so forth.

Hedda feels like a martyr. She thinks she's sacrificing her whole life to please others. But what choice does she have (she says to herself). After all, her father sexually abused her. Her mother was mean. Her sister was the family pet (that sneaky little creep). Her brother got all the glory. Nobody gave her the time of day, nobody gave her love.

It's all their fault, see. Poor Hedda has no choice. As far as she's concerned, she has every right to be angry after all they've done to her. They screwed her over, and now they're gonna pay. Yes, Hedda's unhappy. Sure, she's lonely. And tired from being angry all the time. But what can she do?

They made her mad. They're still treating her bad. She'll just have to stay angry until they change.

Hedda refuses to take responsibility for her own life. It's easier to blame others. Then they're the ones who have to change, not the ragers.

What's wrong here? Simple. *You won't change until you take responsibility for your own actions.* Period. The best way to guarantee your unhappiness is to blame others. The only way to get better is to quit pointing fingers.

Nobody is ruining your life but you.

You might remember a famous line from the old "Pogo" comic strip: "We have met the enemy and he is us." The "enemy" is your avoidance of responsibility.

"I make me mad!" Not *you*. I'm it. If you show up half an hour late and by then my face is purple, that's *me* who made me angry. If I sit and stew about something you said or did, that's *me* who's got a problem, not you. When I convince myself you're thinking of leaving me and then blow sky high, it's *me* who did that to me.

I must take responsibility for my actions. That's the only way I can change. If I make me mad, then I can do something about it. I don't have to wait for you.

Poor Communication Skills

Beverly and Mason are having a disagreement. Bev wants to go to her parents this weekend. Mason wants to stay home. The talk starts calmly. But after a minute or two Mason's in trouble. He just can't say what he wants to say. He can't find the words. Nothing he says ever comes out right.

Mason feels overwhelmed. That's when he gets angry. He sputters, mutters, and roars. He storms out of the house. He grouses and pouts, and then he comes back, still not knowing what to say.

Mason is a poor talker. He's never learned basic communication skills. He can't listen very well. He can't share his feelings. He doesn't know how to speak clearly and directly. He can't state his wants and needs. Mason gets furious at himself and others because he's so frustrated.

Are you like Mason? If so, you'll need to get help learning how to talk and listen better. I'll pass along a few tips during the rest of this book, such as how to make "I" statements. But you'll need to read a book or two on communication or maybe sign up for a class on individual or couples communication.

A Defense Against Other Feelings and Closeness

Anger can be a "cover emotion." It's so loud and strong that it keeps you from noticing anything else.

Your seventeen-year-old son Kevin borrows the car. He's supposed to get home by midnight. You wake up at two in the morning. No Kevin. You're instantly enraged. "Where is that stupid kid. Why, when he gets home I'll let him have it. How dare he do this to me!"

Now your wife wakes up, too. She doesn't look irate, though. She's worried. She'd like to talk with you about her fears. But she doesn't. All you'd do is shout at her, tell her she's a wimp. You'd turn your anger on her.

Aren't you a little bit scared? After all, Kevin is generally reliable. Maybe there's been an accident.

Habitually angry people act like anger is the only legal emotion. Sorry, no fear allowed—you think I'm a weakling? No sadness either—that's too mushy a feeling, I hate it when I cry. No joy or happiness—hey, it's a tough world out there, I don't want to get soft. No shame or guilt—sissy feelings, besides I'm too busy blaming others. Only anger. Anger is the one emotion the rageaholic can handle.

What happens when the rageaholic starts to feel one of these outlawed emotions? Change them, quick. Turn them into anger before anyone sees that you can feel something else. Don't let yourself feel those other things, either. That would be scary.

It seems ridiculous to say, but anger is the only *safe* feeling for the rageaholic. That's another reason it's hard to give up.

Are you ready to look under the covers, to unwrap the rest of your feelings so you can be a whole human being? If not, then you're doing the right thing. Stay angry all the time. You'll never have to deal with the joys and pain of real life.

There's something else that anger hides. That is the desire for closeness, for love. The rageaholic thinks:

> I want to be loved, but it's scary. I feel vulnerable. You can hurt me if I let myself love you. Better to keep you away, keep you at arm's distance. But how?
>
> Ah, yes, with rage. I'll find a thousand reasons to pick fights. I'll drive you away. Good-bye, cruel lover. I hate you. Go away.
>
> Wait! I don't really mean go away. I want you to stay. But I'm afraid to let you get close. That's why I rant and rave. You won't leave me, will you? You know I love you. Please understand me. I'm saying "Go to hell," but it's just a cover.

Do you honestly believe somebody will stick around forever that way? Come on. Let's get real here. The way you keep a lover is by loving them. If you rage at them, they're going to leave.

Partners of angry people tell me they can't take it any more. Yes, they know you really love them. They know the anger is a defense against closeness. But they tell me they can't wait any longer. They're sick and tired of being attacked, bullied, insulted.

If you love someone, show it. Let go of your anger for a while. Maybe you'll get hurt. Maybe you'll be betrayed or abandoned. But, frankly, the chances of being hurt or abandoned are better now, with you acting like a jerk.

Habit

Sheer force of habit is the next major reason people stay angry.

- The sun rises every morning. So does my anger.
- I eat three meals a day. I have two bouts of rage.
- I sleep eight hours a night. I always have angry dreams.
- I work five days a week. I get mad seven out of seven.

Habits are "overlearned" behaviors. That means we don't have to think about what to do. We just do it. Like tying shoelaces. I haven't thought about how to tie a shoelace since about second grade. I'd probably get all confused if I started thinking about it.

Habits are efficient. That's what makes them valuable. It frees us to think about other things. But what if we've developed a "bad" habit? They're hard to change just because we don't think before we act.

Anger is a very bad habit. You get mad all the time without even thinking about it, without making any conscious choices.

Imagine flying on a plane and hearing this announcement from the pilot:

> Welcome aboard, ladies and gentlemen. The good news for today is that I've flown this route over 500 times. I'm so used to it I can fly it with my eyes shut. In fact, that's exactly what I'm planning today, 2,000 miles of automatic flight, all with my eyes shut. I'm confident we will have a wonderful flight.

Now that sure would get your attention, wouldn't it? Habitually angry people go through life that way:

> Attention, ladies and gentleman. I just want to announce that I learned all about life many years ago. I learned to be angry a lot. I was an excellent student, so I've gotten awfully good at anger. It's automatic now, of course. I can get mad about almost anything. I never think about it, either. I'm going through life now with my eyes shut. Thank God for the habit of anger. It sure makes life simple.

For someone with an anger habit, that anger feels normal, familiar, part of the daily routine. What is lost is flexibility. The rageaholic cannot respond differently to different situations—they all call for anger.

A key phrase is "of course I'm angry."

There is no "of course" about anger. There are no automatic reasons to get mad.

Anger is a hard habit to break. The most important thing you'll need to do is to *slow down the whole process*. Take nothing for granted. Think about everything before you act. Don't do anything until you've had time to sort things out. When you catch yourself getting instantly angry, make yourself stop. Ask yourself if there is any good reason—really good reason— for you to be angry right now. Ask yourself if it's just the old habit of anger sneaking up on you again. If it is, stop what you're doing and do something else.

The Anger Rush

Helen has been in trouble most of her life. Today I'm seeing her to help her take a good look at her anger. She's telling me about a recent fight she had with her boyfriend. She got so mad she socked him in the eye. Then he smacked her. They almost broke up. Her head still hurts from the pounding. A pretty big mess—almost a disaster.

Why, then, is Helen smiling? Not a huge smile, mind you. Just a little trace around the corners of her mouth. Let's ask.

> Well, Ron, I'll tell you a secret. I really get off on my anger. The adrenalin rush. It makes me feel high.

I'll tell you a secret: *That anger rush is what keeps a lot of people angry.*

Craig Nakken, in his book, *The Addictive Personality**, says two things that are important here. First, you can become addicted to events, like fighting, not just to substances, like alcohol. The main indicator of an addiction is that you love and trust that event more than anything else.

Some angry people have learned to love and trust anger in this same way. Rage is the old reliable emotion. You can always count on it to get you high.

**The Addictive Personality: Understanding Compulsion in Our Lives*, by Craig Nakken, published in 1988 by Harper & Row, San Francisco, CA.

Second, Nakken talks about how addicts substitute intensity for intimacy. That means they don't want a close and safe relationship. That's far too tame. The addict wants strong feelings.

Strong anger is exciting. Shouting and fighting get the blood flowing. They make you feel alive. Take away the fighting and you feel dull, depressed, bored.

Nobody talks about the anger rush. It's one of the best kept secrets around. But it's there, for both men and women.

> No, no, Ron, not me. I don't do that. Why, anger makes me feel awful. I don't feel good when I get mad.

OK, I believe you. But that's not the point. You may feel good or bad when you get an anger rush. Either way, it's a *strong* feeling, an overpowering sensation, intense. That's what I'm talking about.

Ever hear the term "excited misery"? That's what many rageaholics have in their life—excitement coupled with misery.

I believe a lot of people stay angry because they don't want to give up the intensity of feeling that it provides. You can teach them communication skills for the next hundred years. But what good will that do if they don't use those skills? And the reason they stay angry is so they can keep getting high.

Some very angry people are emotional junkies. *They have become emotionally addicted to their anger.* They may tell you they don't like it, and that may be true. But they *need* it. And that's why it's so hard for them to let go of their anger.

What exactly is it that is so addictive about the anger rush? I think it's the feeling of being intensely alive.

What happens if you take away this feeling? Boredom, restlessness, emptiness. Life feels stale and dull. Depression.

And then what? Relapse. Returning to the anger just to feel again.

So here's the problem. You want to feel good. You want energy, power, excitement. Mostly, you want to *feel*. Otherwise, you face boredom and depression. But by now you rely on your anger to feel. You've become emotionally dependent upon your anger. It's time to change.

Every beginning starts with an ending. We give up one thing to get something better. And that's the way it is with anger. You have to say goodbye to the rage. To the rush. To the emotional addiction. You can't have it and lead a normal life.

You can't change your life until you make a commitment to quit seeking the anger rush. Are you ready? What do you think your life will be like without those moments of intensity?

> OK, Ron. I'll do it. I'll give up the anger rush. But what can I replace it with? I want to feel alive. I'm not just going to quit raging and die. What's the trade-off?

I'll be honest. I can't offer you a complete replacement for the anger rush. The intensity is simply not part of normal life. The same goes for cocaine highs, the sexual surge of the cruising sex addict, even the power surge of the bulimic throwing up in the toilet. You have to give up extremes in order to have a decent life.

But I can offer you something completely different and better—a whole new way of life. It will be like trading in an old bicycle for a new car. You can achieve calmness, peace of mind, happiness, healthy relationships, a whole range of normal feelings instead of a bucket full of rage. That's my offer. Trade in that old bicycle called rage and step into a modern vehicle that will get you a lot farther.

Summary

We've studied six main reasons people stay unreasonably angry: the desire for power and control, avoiding responsibility for their own life, poor communication skills, defending against other feelings and closeness, habit, and the anger rush.

Please review these six reasons. Which are the strongest for you? Are there others? There might be. I've only listed the ones I run into most often.

Now what? The main thing is for you to start working on these six things. You decide which is the most important. Or ask others to help you decide. Then get to work. You can't just sit there and hope life will get better. Start making the changes hinted at in this chapter now, and today your life will start to improve.

Meanwhile, keep reading. We've still got a long ways to go in this book.

4

The Anger and Violence Ladder

Habitually angry people are great athletes. You can see them out there practicing every day. Grunting at others. Shouting out discouragement. Running away from their problems.

Their best sport is ladder climbing. On the next page is a picture of their favorite ladder.

Let's climb the ladder together now. I'm sure it's one you've walked up before. But this time we'll go slowly enough to study each step.

Step One: Sneaky Anger

The first rung on the ladder is the easiest to climb. You don't even have to admit you're mad at anybody.

The goal of sneaky anger is to totally frustrate somebody. Here's one way. Just *forget* what they want you to do.

> Oh yeah, Bob, you're right. I was supposed to put the money in the bank. Now we're overdrawn again. Sorry.

Sorry? No way. It's the third time this spring Helen's forgotten something important. Each time she was secretly angry at

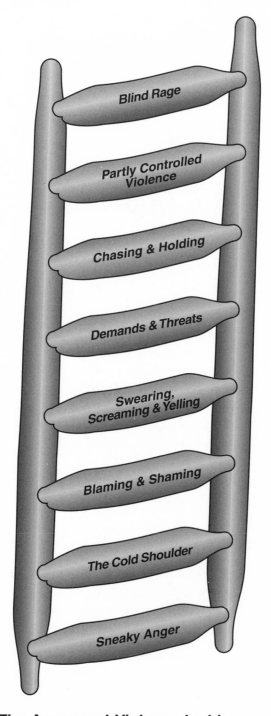

The Anger and Violence Ladder

Bob. But Helen never said a thing. Instead, she found a sneaky way to punish him.

How about the old "yeah, but" routine?

Will: I know it's my job to mow the lawn this week, but there's no gas in the tank.

Melody: I'll get you the gas. Then you can do it.

Will: Yeah, but we really can't afford a trip into town today.

Melody: Oh, here's some gas, right over here. Now you can get going.

Will: Yeah, but now the sun's out and the grass is too dry.

"Yeah, but," "yeah, but", "yeah, but" really means no, no, no. It's another form of sneaky anger.

Playing Dumb

Henry teaches engineering at the local college. But try asking him when he'll pick up his kids for a weekend visit. "Gee, I don't know. It's so hard to figure stuff like that out. I've never been able to live by a schedule." He's never missed a classroom lecture, though. Here's the translation:

Angie, you divorced me. Now I'm going to make you pay. I'll act stupid and drive you crazy. Acting dumb gives me the power to hurt you every other weekend. I like that.

Leaving Things Out

Oh, Fred, didn't I tell you I'm going gambling at the casino Saturday? Silly me! Guess I'll miss your party. Sorry.

There's that nasty word "sorry" again. Why do people say they're sorry when they are actually angry? So nobody can blame them. If Fred gets angry now, Beth can look hurt.

Why, Fred, I don't understand. Why are you angry
at me? I didn't do anything.

That's the sneaky anger strategy. Act innocent but do
something to frustrate the hell out of somebody. *It's not what
you do. It's what you don't do. That's how you show your anger.*
Leave things out. Don't complete your jobs, especially jobs
that others depend on you for. Maybe then they'll leave you
alone.

Whining

One more common sneaky anger pattern is whining, low-
level complaining, grumbling under your breath.
"What's that you said, Tommy?"
"Nothing." Grumble, grumble, mutter, moan.
"Something wrong, Tommy?"
"I said nothing's wrong. Grrrrrrrrrrrrrrrrrr, mnnnnnnn-
nnnnn."
Tommy sounds like distant thunder. But nothing's wrong.
Sure.
Sneaky anger is only the first step on the ladder. There
are still seven more rungs to climb.

Step Two: The Cold Shoulder

I'm mad at you and I'm not gonna talk about it. So
there! That'll show you.

Obviously ignoring people is a little more direct than
sneaky anger. At least people know you're angry. Of course,
they may not know about what. They'll just have to guess,
won't they? You're sure not going to tell them.
This is a form of punishment. You're out to hurt somebody.
You're angry.
It's the ancient art of *shunning*. Hector broke the rules.
He prayed for rain on Tuesday. Nobody prays for rain until
Wednesday. It offends the gods. So let's kick Hector out of
the village. If he tries to come back, nobody can talk to him.
Make him suffer.

Doesn't that sound dumb? How about this one? Herman broke the rules. He got a girl pregnant. Now they're getting married.

I'm not going. I won't talk to him ever again—won't see the baby. He's out of my life forever.

Silence is a weapon for some angry people. It's a way of telling others they're bad. But face facts. Giving someone the cold shoulder is poor communication. You'll never solve your problems like that.

Maybe you're too angry with your friend to talk right now. You're afraid you'll blow up. OK, take a time-out (see Chapter 6). That's not the same as punishing him or her with your silence. You're going to have to learn how to talk when you're angry.

Step Three: Blaming and Shaming

This form of anger is more direct. The message is this:

There's something wrong with you. I know it. I'm gonna say it. I want you to feel bad because I'm angry with you.

Angry people often blame others for their problems. *You* gave me a headache. *You* made me mad. It's all *your* fault. You, you, you.

It's your fault, so I have a right to blame you. Let's take a few hours to discuss your weaknesses. You're lazy. You're fat. You're dumb. You're too smart for your own good. You're a coward. You're a nobody. You don't make enough money. You work too hard.

In our book, *Letting Go of Shame*, my wife Pat and I write about five shaming messages. Shaming messages tell others they are bad. The messages say there's something really wrong; usually something the person can't fix. The five messages are:

- You're no good
- You're not good enough
- You're unlovable

- You don't belong
- You shouldn't be

These are terrible, angry things to say. Even in a whisper. Besides, who are you to judge?

Blaming and shaming are mean things to do. They make others feel awful.

So what, you say.

> Why should that stop me? Hey, I'm mad at Judy. I want her to feel miserable. That's why I call her a slut and a whore. I know exactly what I'm doing. And it works. I can make her cry whenever I want.

Great! But after she's done crying she calls you a total failure in life (that's the one thing she can say that really gets to you). Then she stays mad and hurt for a week. And your son Jerry overheard you and won't go to the game with you. And your four-year-old Trudy wants you to explain why you made Mommy cry.

Blaming and shaming are anger weapons. Sometimes they work, sometimes they don't. They often backfire. Then you get blamed and shamed back. And that's when you climb another rung on the anger ladder.

Step Four: Swearing, Screaming, and Yelling

Jack ordered his three-year-old stepdaughter Ruth to eat all her dinner.

"No, I won't." Ruth refused.

"Please be a good girl and eat your dinner."

"No, I won't."

"Then you're a naughty girl. You're being bad. You're a bad little girl."

"I don't care! I'm not hungry."

Jack was speechless for a few seconds. Then he started to turn purple. Suddenly he was shouting in Ruth's face. "You fucking brat. I hate you. I hate your sister too." On and on he went—yelling, cursing, screaming. His voice rose higher and higher. He didn't stop even after Ruth began sobbing. His wife Trudy, running in from the kitchen, had to pull him away.

Jack has a foul mouth. He swears at home, at work, at church. He says it's a bad habit he picked up from his dad. He tries to quit swearing every once in a while, but not very hard.

He says he never shouts. He's just "loud" a lot. Very loud.

Tiny Julia is a screamer. You can hear her a block away when she blows. "Shhh," her boyfriend says. "Don't you 'shhh' me, you shithead," Julia yells. She'll scream all she wants. The neighbors can just go ahead and call the cops again.

Why? Tell me one thing that only makes sense when you shout. Since when does yelling make you sound smarter?

Screaming, cursing, and shouting do exactly one thing. They make you look stupid. Real stupid. Not that you're a dummy, mind you. You're just acting like one when you develop a case of foul mouthitis.

"But I need to let off steam, Ron. Besides, isn't it good for your health to explode once in a while?"

First, you don't *need* to let off steam. You *want* to. There's a big difference. You won't die if you talk softer. You won't get lockjaw.

Second, exploding is *not* good for your health. It's generally damaging.

Third, if you want to shout, go ahead—but in the woods out back or in the basement behind closed doors. Why should anybody else have to listen to that garbage?

Fourth, you've got a big problem with anger, remember. You don't have a normal relationship with anger. You don't swear a little. You don't shout a little. You swear a lot. You shout a lot. Too much. Way too much.

Swearing, screaming, and yelling are signs you're losing control of your anger. You need to tell yourself to stop immediately. There's no excuse for a foul mouth or a loud mouth. None.

If you don't stop, you'll soon be climbing the anger ladder again.

Step Five: Demands and Threats

It's starting to look ugly now, real ugly. All that sneaky anger, the cold shoulders, the blaming and shaming, the swearing and screaming. And you're still not in control. Time to up the ante.

> Damn it, I asked you nicely to turn down the stereo. But no, you didn't do it, did you. Well, now you better shut it off, or you're gonna pay.

Do it or else. That's the message. Do it or else I'll get really mad. Do it or else I'll hit you. Do it or else no sex for a week. Do it or else I'm outta here. Do it or else I'll take the kids away and you'll never see them again. Do it or else I'll tell everybody you're crazy. Do it or else.

Remember that sad line from the old Rolling Stones song? "You can't always get what you want, you can't always get what you want." Well, don't tell that to the habitually angry person.

"What do you mean, Ron? Nobody better try to stop me."

That reminds me of a story.

The Mighty Rolf

There once lived a mighty giant named Rolf. Rolf was a rageaholic. He was strong. He was tough. He was mean. He was a bully.

One day Rolf the rageaholic met a beautiful princess.

"I demand a million dollars," he said. "Pay up or else."

"Or else what?" asked the princess, who didn't seem all that scared.

"Or else I'll huff, and I'll puff, and I'll blow your palace down!" Well, this princess knew all about big nasty rageaholics. She'd been married to one when she was younger. Back then she lived in a palace made of straw. Man, did he make a mess of it. After she threw him out she built a new palace. This one was made with two-by-sixes, reinforced walls, and dragon-breath rated insulation.

"Take a hike," she told Rolf.

Rolf didn't like that at all. So he huffed and he puffed all night. He huffed and he puffed all day. He got red in the face. Then he turned blue. "Gee, I thought I could make anybody do what I wanted if I threatened them enough," he complained.

"Not me," replied the princess. "Now get out of here before I send for my army." And he did.

Step Six: Chasing and Holding

Physical violence begins when you take away another person's freedom.

Penny's mad because Bill forgot to switch the wet laundry to the dryer. She corners him in the den watching TV. She follows him to the kitchen. The more she talks, the angrier she gets. His apologies don't stop her. "I don't have to listen to this abuse," he says. "I'm taking a ride in the car." But it's not that easy to escape. Penny jumps in her car to chase after him.

Douglas is furious with Ellen. He's certain she's been flirting with the guys at work. He's jealous. He's been grilling her for an hour. Finally Ellen's had enough. She gets up to leave. But he won't let her go. Not until he's done talking. What's her hurry, anyhow? Does she have a secret meeting with a man? He grabs her wrist and hangs on to it tightly so she can't get away.

Penny is chasing Bill. Douglas is holding (restraining) Ellen. Both are taking away somebody's freedom. This is violence.

I hear a lot of excuses in this area. "No, I'm not violent. I never hit anyone. I just want them to listen, so I won't let them leave." Wrong! You're taking away their choices, aren't you. That's violence.

Here's a dictionary definition of violence: *violence is any unjust or unfair use of force or power against another's rights.* Violent acts injure others. Chasing and holding take away a person's rights to choose where they want to be and what they want to do.

Angry people get really steamed when anyone tries to tell them what to do. Make them wait around and they get annoyed. And don't chase after them unless you're ready for a fight.

So how about everybody playing on a level field? It's not OK for others to chase or hold you. So stop chasing and holding them.

Step Seven: Partly Controlled Violence

It's major-league frustration time. Those *fools* just keep giving you a hard time. You started out trying to be nice. Then you raised your voice. Then you threatened and bullied. And then you followed them around like a lonely puppy trying to make them agree with you. Now you're done playing games.

Shove. Pull. Pinch. Slap. Hit. Kick. Choke. Knife. Shoot.

The goal is power and control, to make them do what you want, to show them who's boss.

I call this *partly controlled* violence. It's controlled because you're attacking others on purpose. You know what you're doing, even though later you might claim it was an accident. You plan to stop when you get your way.

But violence is like a caged tiger snarling at her keeper. You can never completely control her. Sooner or later she'll strike. And that's when you lose your head.

> What happened? One minute Sally and I were goofing around. Wrestling. Then she slapped me on the face. I got really mad and punched her. I went berserk.

Or

> I was spanking my kid Joey. He sassed me. I figured I'd teach him a lesson he wouldn't forget. But then I smacked him right in the stomach. He couldn't breathe and I got scared.

Violence is dangerous. Once the cork is out of the bottle it's hard to put it back. That's why *there's no such thing as a little violence.*

There is no reason for violence in everyday life. (OK, if a crazed lunatic attacks your partner and kids, do your thing. Defend them. Be a hero. But until then, quit acting like everybody is a raving madman.)

You're in pretty sad shape if you go around hurting people. Can't you think of anything else? Have you lost the ability to talk? Do something now, before you kill someone.

There are two important things wrong with partly controlled violence:

- It's a crude way to get your way—an act of desperation that makes you look awful and ugly—and it usually doesn't work very well.

- It often leads to uncontrolled violence—to blind rage.

Step Eight: Blind Rage

My God. The last thing I remember was charging at Jack. He says I was cursing and practically foaming at the mouth. I guess I spat on him. I bit. Jack's got scratches all over his arms. His new nickname for me is Claw.

Normally anger follows a predictable path, like electricity through a wire. It starts in the "old" brain (the limbic system). It pours out of there ready to help you fight or flee. But then it gets channeled through the "new" brain (the parts of the brain that developed more recently among human beings and help us use reason) where the energy can be controlled. Your new brain tells you what the problem is, what to do about it, how to put the anger to good use.

Severe anger is a problem, though. The new brain can be overpowered. It can't handle that much anger. It needs protection. That's when the new brain flips its circuit breakers. It switches off your conscious thoughts.

Wonderful. You won't go crazy now, but there's nothing left to control your anger. It turns into blind rage, which is usually a mixture of tremendous anger and terror.

The goal of blind rage is to destroy. That's why it's so dangerous. Kill or be killed.

Extremely angry people go into many blind rages. Like a pump that's been primed, they're ready. The difference is they squirt rage instead of water.

You can't wait until you're out of control to seek help. It's too late by then. By then you may have done something you'll regret the rest of your life.

Summary

What a nasty ladder! Sneaky anger. Cold shoulder. Blaming and shaming. Swearing, screaming, and yelling. Demands and threats. Chasing and holding. Partly controlled violence. Blind rage. Up and up you climb.

Where do you go from here? There's only one choice: down the ladder. We'll take the next three chapters to show you how.

Are you ready?

PART II

Action

5

Fish or Cut Bait—
It's Time To Make
a Promise

This is it. You can only learn about your anger so long. Then it's time to do something about it. It's time to change.

Real change begins with a promise to yourself. A promise to do whatever you need to do. To think in new ways. To act in new ways. And, for the angry person, even to feel differently.

You'll need courage—the courage to start a new life and the guts to stick it out. You'll need the strength to say no to dozens of anger invitations, no matter how tempting.

You'll need to be honest with yourself so you don't fall back into denial of your anger. You must be willing to admit your mistakes, and to correct them.

You'll need to use your brain. Recovering from too much anger doesn't just happen. You have to think up some new ways to do things.

You'll need help. Don't try to do this alone. Get help from people you trust. Get help from "normies" who handle their anger better than you.

Make a promise to yourself. A real one. A deep pledge. A vow. It's called a commitment.

A commitment to what?

The Goal

To stay calm. That's the goal.

> Calm.   Peaceful.   Relaxed.
> At ease.   Composed.   Patient.
> Quiet.   Cool-headed.   Steady.
> Serene.   Tranquil.   Poised.

Think of a still pond, with just a hint of a breeze to keep you cool.

Picture yourself smiling as your children play, simply enjoying them.

Imagine yourself as the person others can count on to keep your cool in stressful situations. You!

Hear yourself telling others, "Hey, no big deal. I'm not mad" (and meaning it).

That's for you when you give up your excessive anger. That's the hope and the promise. It's not easy, of course. Nothing that really matters is.

Two Kinds of Calm

There are two kinds of calm. They're both important. You'll need both. The first kind of calm means almost never getting angry. The second kind of calm means learning how to express yourself better, even when angry.

Calm = Almost Never Getting Angry

Staying calm means saying no to almost every anger invitation.

Bill is a recovering angry man. Here's why he won't let himself get mad.

> Ron, I used to be angry all the time. I woke up mad, I stayed mad all day, I went to bed mad. I hurt a lot of people. I could've killed someone. Or been killed. I had to quit. But it's always there, waiting to take

over. I can't afford to get angry, even once. For me, I always find a different way. I won't even let myself get annoyed, because I know where that leads. I refuse to go through that misery again.

Bill is like the alcoholic who knows he can't have even one drink. He's promised himself a new life. He's willing to give up his anger for that new life.

Sure, you say. The poor guy must be a human doormat. People will walk over him. He can't defend himself without anger.

No, it's not that way. He's doing fine. Bill's no wimp. He's stronger now than he was before. Nobody pushes him around. His life is better, not worse.

Bill has made a choice to give up his anger. He feels a whole lot better without it. Now he can enjoy his friends, his job, his family, his life. He's happy now. He's found some inner peace. Anger is a luxury he cannot afford.

Bill has found an answer to his problem. He's traded in his rage for a new chance in life.

Calm = Learning To Express Yourself Better, Even When Angry

There's another way, though. Listen to Becky.

Ron, I hated my rages. It wasn't the anger, it was the loss of control. I'd go ballistic over little things. Then I decided that being mad was no excuse for going nuts. I've made a promise, but not like Bill. My goal is to stay in control, even when I'm angry."

Becky can handle a little anger once in a while. Not too much, not too often. Mostly, she has to remember to keep her anger under control. She has to remember to talk instead of scream; ask, not demand.

Anger is heat. We get hotheaded. We simmer, and then we boil over. We steam. We can take our anger temperature as shown on the next page.

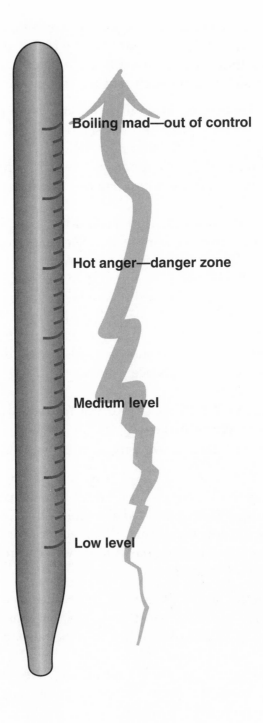

Boiling mad—out of control

Hot anger—danger zone

Medium level

Low level

Bill tries to keep his anger at or near the bottom of the thermometer. He has to do this to survive.

Becky can manage low-level anger. She can even handle medium levels if she is very careful. She can't let herself get really mad, though. When that happens she always loses control. She goes from "hot anger" to "boiling mad."

Bill is like an alcoholic who can never drink again. Becky is more like someone who eats way too much. She needs to learn how to eat better.

Bill says no to almost all of his anger. Becky says no to the times when she gets too angry. She says no to the times she stays angry too long.

Bill's promise: *no more anger* for me. I can't afford even one time.

Becky's promise: *no more anger binges*. No more extreme anger.

The Promise You Need To Make Today

Relax. You don't have to make either Bill's or Becky's promise. Not yet. Those are lifetime goals. You're not ready for them. You couldn't keep either one. Here's yours:

I promise to stay calm one whole day.

That's all. Twenty-four hours. No blowups. No yelling. No lecturing. No raging. Twenty-four hours of peace and quiet.

I'm not talking about stuffing your anger for twenty-four hours and then getting twice as mad tomorrow. That's useless. I'm not talking about pretending to others you're calm when you're going crazy inside. That's phony.

Calm means *calm*. Quiet. It means *you choose to let go of your anger* for a while. Call off the dogs for a day. Take off your armor. Lay down your weapons for twenty-four hours. Remember, you can always pick them back up. Nobody can stop you from getting angry.

Put your anger on the shelf for one day. See what happens. What do you have to lose?

Six Steps To Help You Keep Your Promise

Promises, promises. Easy to make. Hard to keep. Why should this one be any different? It can be, though. You can keep this promise. If you're willing to do a little work in advance, that is. There are six things you can do that will help you stay calm for one whole day.

1. Tell people about your promise. "Sure, I want to keep my promise. But what if I mess up? I better not tell anybody so I won't be embarrassed."

You might as well admit you're going to fail when you think like that. You've got to believe in yourself or you're lost before you start.

Forget caution. This is an important goal. It's your chance to start a new life. Besides, so what if you mess up? It's not the end of the world. You'll feel bad, which is good. You'll need to take some time to figure out what you did wrong. And then you'll just have to make another promise. Sooner or later you'll get it right.

Tell your friends. Tell the world. Most important, tell the people you get mad at the most.

> Betty, kids, I just want you to know I'm making a
> promise to stay calm today. I'm tired of yelling so
> much. I'll do my best not to pick any fights today.

No bullshit allowed. *Do not* tell them they have to help you stay calm. It's not their job, it's yours.

Secrets make you sick. Don't keep this a secret. Let it out.

2. Ask for support. "Betty, I sure could use your support. This is scary stuff. I might need someone to talk to. Can I come to you if it gets tough?"

Betty has the right to say no. Don't ask a yes-or-no question unless you can accept either answer. If she says no, ask others. There are lots of people who want to help. Helping you may be good for them.

Look around you. Do you know people who handle their anger well? Is there someone who stays calm when others aren't? AA says stick with the winners. You need to hang around folks who aren't angry a lot. Avoid other rageaholics, especially now. They can't help you much. And they might encourage you to blow up.

You need support. Get it. This is no time for false pride.

3. No "only ifs" or "yeah, buts." No bargaining allowed. Nothing like, "Well, OK, I'll be nice *if* you are. But if you're not, then I quit." You're bargaining when there's nothing to bargain with. You're the one with the problem. Only you can change what you do. You're just setting yourself up to fail again—and to have somebody else to blame.

"Sorry, Ron. I really do want to quit, but I have to wait until Mars and Venus are lined up just right. Then I can turn my anger into love." Isn't that about the weakest excuse you ever heard? It's a "yeah, but" of the weirdest kind. And it's not much different from those I hear a lot.

"Yeah, Ron, I want to be calm, but I can't start today. You see, I have a bad cold and that makes me grumpy." Or,

"I'm too anxious."

"It's Thursday and Thursdays are always tough."

"Today is a bad one at work."

"It's the kid's birthday and you know how much they yell" (so you're gonna yell right back at them, right?).

Face it. You've been making up excuses forever. There's always a reason to get angry when you're looking for one.

Today is the day to start. Right now. No more excuses. No more false promises. No more blaming others. Or are you sitting there this very moment thinking up another reason to put it off?

4. Remember the bad stuff. Please go back to the anger pie in Chapter 1. Look over all the trouble your anger has brought you: family problems, arguments at work, damaged or lost friendships, accidents or medical concerns, money you threw away when angry, hassles with the law, loss of control, becoming "mean-spirited."

Feeling bad is good for now. This time you're feeling bad *before* you mess up, not after. You can use the bad feeling to make a stronger promise.

You'd like to feel pride in yourself again. You can, starting today, but only by making and keeping that promise to stay calm. Get your act together. It does wonders for you. It changes shame and guilt into self-respect.

5. Plan ahead. Take a peek at the next twenty-four hours. Is there anything coming up that you need to prepare for? Things that you would usually get mad about? Maybe silly Aunt Matilda is coming with her yappy poodle Lucifer. Oh, how you hate that dog! Or your partner is planning on painting the walls and expects you to help. Or the boss and his crew of butt-kissers will be inspecting your part of the plant. Or your daughter Mandy is having a sleep-over with her three best (and noisiest) friends.

What can you do to get ready so you don't break your promise? You want to stay calm. How can you do that? This is called planning ahead.

I can tell how serious people are by how much they plan. The least serious ones say, "Oh, maybe I'll figure something out. I'm sure I'll think of something." Sure they will. No way!

The men and women who really want to change are different. They think. They talk it over. They come up with a realistic plan.

"I'll take a walk if Aunt Matilda and Lucifer both start barking at me."

"I'll tell him I'll only paint in the morning. I need some time for myself."

"I'll mind my own business when the boss comes. If others kiss ass, that's their choice. I feel good about mine."

"I need to talk with Mandy and her friends when they get here. They can gab all they want until midnight, but then it's settle down or I'll take the others home."

Are these good plans? They look good. Each is simple

and clear. They only depend on your action, not somebody else's.

You don't quit being angry with wishes. You need to think ahead, to plan, to try new things that help you stay calm.

6. Set positive goals. This isn't just about stopping something bad—your rage. It's about beginning something good. A new start. A new life. A normal life. Pride and self-respect are two positive goals already mentioned. Other goals are:

- A family without fear

- A partner who wants to be around you

- Friends and relatives who enjoy your company

- Peace of mind

- A sense of hope instead of misery

- Better health

- Fewer arguments at work or school (maybe even enjoying being around your co-workers)

- Money to spend on good stuff, not to replace broken windows and telephones

- Friends who stay friends

- No more Dr. Jekyll and Mr. Hyde—stable feelings

- Feeling in control of your life

A whole busload of feelings can be yours. Happiness, fear, sadness, all the feelings you've hidden so long under a blanket of anger.

Most of all, *freedom*. You will no longer be a prisoner of your own anger.

Instead of My Anger, I Could Have . . .

You're having a dream. You're in a jail cell, but dressed in civilian clothes. You feel heavy. And you're carrying a huge rock on your shoulders. You're tired, very tired. You just want to lay down that rock.

The warden walks up to your cell. He's got the key. You've served your time, he says. Enough is enough. You can be free. All you have to do is put down that rock. Then you can walk out of the cell.

How much do you want your freedom? Will you take the rock off your shoulders? Today?

What About the Long Term—Beyond the Next Twenty-Four Hours

Remember those two kinds of calm.

- Calm = almost never getting angry.

- Calm = learning how to express yourself better, even when angry.

Those are the long-term goals. You'll need both kinds of calm.

You'll need to set a goal of almost never getting angry. That makes sense, doesn't it? After all, you've been angry way too long. You have to let go of that need to get mad.

You will never have a "normal" relationship with anger. It's too dangerous, too powerful. You have to say good-bye to it. Your anger is not a friend anymore.

You'll have to say no to lots of anger invitations—to more than some other people who don't have your problems with anger.

You'll also need to learn how to express yourself better, even when you get angry. You'll need tools. We'll be talking about tools—fair fighting, "I" statements, respectful communication, sharing your feelings without hurting people—in Chapters 6 and 7.

Summary

A recovering angry person is someone who has made a promise. The promise is to stay calm for twenty-four hours.

To recover, you must become someone who wants to almost never get angry. But when you do get angry, you'll want to learn good ways to talk. There are ways to say what you think without hurting others.

Six steps help you keep the twenty-four hour promise:

- Tell others

- Ask for support

- No "only ifs" or "yeah, buts"

- Remember the bad stuff

- Plan ahead

- Set positive goals

Are you ready?

The Promise

I, _____, promise

to stay calm for twenty-four hours, beginning at _____ a.m./

p.m. on _____(day), _____(year).

Your signature _____

Witness _____

Now let's go on to the next chapter. It's on how to quit being violent.

6

Climbing Down the Ladder, Part 1— No More Violence or Threats

You've got to get off the anger ladder. Not to be nice. Not because others tell you to. *You've got to get off because anger is ruining your life.*

Imagine you're about to explore a wilderness. You need a guide. But the first man to show up is a rageaholic. He picks a fight with you. He threatens to beat up your friend. He whips out a gun and shoots his partner.

Would you hire this guy? Very angry people would. Actually, they already have. Every day they use their anger as a guide.

> Let's get going, buddy. We're gonna really work up a rage today. First, see that ladder over there? Start climbing. That's right, all the way up. Then a break-fast brawl. By noon we'll make enemies of the natives. And by supper you'll be so mad you won't talk to anybody. Then we'll start a forest fire and burn down our own tent. How's that sound?"

Is this the way you want to live? If not, fire the guide. Get out of the anger wilderness before you're lost in there forever.

The way out begins by climbing down the anger ladder.

Where do you start? Simple. *Stop the worst first.* Begin at the top of the ladder and work your way down. Get off the top steps before you do any more damage. End the violence.

Eleven rules will help you climb down the ladder. I'll list them here. Then we'll look at them more carefully in these next two chapters.

1. Take time-outs to stop your violence.

2. Wipe that frown off your face and relax.

3. Quit trying to control others.

4. Accept difference.

5. Ask, don't demand.

6. Reward, don't punish or threaten.

7. Speak quietly and don't swear.

8. Be responsible for everything you say and do.

9. Treat others with respect.

10. Tell others what bothers you. Be direct, specific, and polite.

11. Use "I" statements.

Safety First—Stopping Violence

Harry gets home just in time to see a strange man leaving his house. He's a very jealous man. Harry's ex-wife had an affair, so he immediately assumes his girlfriend Tess is cheating. Instant rage. Stomach on fire. Blood pounding through his temples. Harry's always had a short fuse and he's already reaching for the match.

Last year Harry would have charged into the house. He'd accuse. He'd threaten. He wouldn't believe Tess's explanation, no matter how reasonable. He'd go ballistic. He'd break things, punch the walls, terrify her. Slap her around. Beat her. Threaten to rape her.

Not this time. Harry's made a promise to himself to end the violence. He knows he can't go in that house. He has to take a time-out.

Rule One To Control Your Anger: Take a Time-out To Stop the Violence

There is only one thing to do when you're this close to an explosion—take a time-out. Leave the scene until you can cool down. This isn't the time to try to solve problems. You are too hot to think straight. Your angry body has taken over. Your old brain is in control.

Warning: Simply walking away from someone you're angry at won't work. You've got to do things during the time-out that will cool you down.

Here's what a good time-out looks like:

You realize you're close to exploding. Rages don't just happen. They're not like a lightning bolt from the blue. They're predictable. There are always a few warning signs. You need to learn yours. **Body signals** like sudden sweating, your gut tightening, or a surge of adrenalin. **Thoughts** such as "That's it. No more. I can't stand it" or "She can't say that to me. I hate her." **Actions** like pacing the floor, making fists, raising your voice. If you catch yourself doing this stuff and you can't stop immediately, you must take a time-out.

You leave. Tell the other person that you're really upset. Tell him or her you've got to leave before you hurt someone or break something. Promise to return when you can talk without losing your temper. By the way, it's important to keep your promise. A time-out is different from running away.

Go somewhere safe where you can calm down. Go sit in your car or on a bench in the park. Your workshop in the garage, a rummage sale, a movie, an AA meeting are other possibilities. It's usually best to go alone, never with people who will pour fuel on the fire. If you're driving there, be careful. The hospital is a lousy place to read the rest of this book!

Do things to help you calm down. Slowly drink a cup of *decaffeinated* coffee (caffeine causes restlessness and irritability). Or take a brisk walk, read an interesting book, practice relaxation. Vigorous activity is OK, but avoid aggressive things like watching a violent film. The goal is to calm down physically, emotionally, and mentally.

Let yourself relax. Let go of that out-of-control feeling. Take your time. I'll say more about relaxation soon.

After a while you may be ready to return. First ask yourself one question. Can I go back now and talk calmly no matter what others say or do? Even if they are angry or upset? If not, don't go back yet. You're just setting yourself up for another round of fights.

Return. Talk with the others about what happened. Stay calm. Go back to the original problem. This time keep your head while you are talking. You'll feel better just knowing you took a good time-out. You helped keep everybody safe.

You Can Do More To Prevent Violence
Time-outs help tremendously, but they are not enough. They are the last line of defense.

If there were a football team named Anger Control, Joe Time-Out would play free safety. He roams around way at the back of the field, the only thing between your anger and disaster. But that guy needs help. He can't do it alone. Where's the rest of the team?

The rest of the team is up closer to where the play begins. Their job is to cut off your anger earlier, before you even begin to lose control.

Each of the other players has a special job. One checks out your thoughts. His job is to stop you from thinking in ways that make you mad. I'll talk more about him in a special chapter (Chapter 8). Another keeps a careful eye on the adrenalin rush that goes with rage. I've already mentioned him. A third has the job of looking at your actions. He tries to stop you when you do things that get you into trouble.

Men and women in AA have a saying: "If you hang around a barber shop, sooner or later you'll get your hair cut." That's why they stay out of taverns. It's the same with anger. If you make a fist, sooner or later you'll hit somebody. If you get in someone's face, sooner or later there'll be a fight. If you go looking for trouble, you'll find it.

Want to be on the team? You can. Make a list of the most common things you say, do, and think that trigger your rage—not what others say, think, or do. Stick with your own stuff. Then *stop* saying, doing, and thinking those things and *start* saying, doing, and thinking something else. It's pretty simple. You just need to change a few of the ways you do things.

You're almost ready to climb down the ladder a rung. But I've got one more recommendation. Get help! Go to a counselor or a therapist who does a lot of anger counseling. You might find someone who specializes in your problem—a therapist who runs a program for spouse beaters, or a counselor who works with parents who hit their kids. That's another way to protect yourself and the people you love.

Rule Two To Control Your Anger: Wipe That Frown Off Your Face and Relax

Relaxation techniques are important for anyone with a serious anger problem. The reason is simple: your body can't both fight and relax at the same time. Most angry people don't realize how tense they are. But they are. Their tension is a setup to get mad.

Let's start at the top, with your face. How often have you heard something like this: "Gee, you sure look angry today. What's wrong?" To which you answer: "Nothing. Why are you always saying I look angry? Are you trying to make me mad?"

The reason people think you're angry is the look on your face. Go to a mirror and take a peek. Do you see the slightly clenched jaw? The glare in your eyes (sometimes called "hard eyes")? The eyebrows edging toward each other like they're trying to meet at your nose? Or perhaps you can hear the loudness or hint of sarcasm in your voice? Or the extra soft whisper that only comes when you are barely holding in your anger.

Your face and voice are announcing your anger. So is your body. Notice the tension in your shoulders and back. The ache in your gut. How easily your hands turn into fists. The foot tapping. Pacing around. The general tightness. The unnatural breathing, sometimes very shallow, sometimes too deep.

All this happens without your knowledge. Your body and face have developed some bad habits. They tense up a lot. They're preparing you for the next fight. That's why people think you're always angry. Because your anger has gotten stored up in your face and body. The message is this: "Come on, I'm ready for a fight. Just give me an excuse."

That's why you need to relax. Not just in the middle of an argument, either. You need to learn to have less tension in your face and body.

Relaxation is a skill. It's something that you can learn. I'll give you a few ideas here, the kind you can use quickly, but I recommend you do some reading. (I suggest *The Relaxation and Stress Reduction Workbook**.) Or get some training.

Soften your eyes. Quit glaring, staring, or squinting. Instead, let the small muscles around your eyes relax. Every time you start to tense up, go right back to your eyes. Make it a habit.

Breathe deeply. Take ten deep, slow breaths, counting them out loud or to yourself.

---

* *The Relaxation and Stress Reduction Workbook*, by Martha Davis, Elizabeth Robbins, and Matthew McKay, published in 1988 by New Harbinger Publications in Oakland, CA.

Talk normally. Check out your voice. Find your normal speed, loudness, and pitch. If you whisper when you get tense or angry, speak up. If you get loud, quiet down.

Tighten up a few muscles, then relax them. Do this with the ones that seem most tight. Breathe calmly as you do this.

Think relaxing thoughts. Repeat these thoughts to yourself, for example, "I will relax right now" and "I can stay in control here. Just relax."

Relaxation can help you with your anger. But don't wait until you're going ballistic. What good will ten deep breaths do then? A little, maybe. But you'd be better off taking those breaths earlier, before you start losing control.

Rule Three To Control Your Anger: Quit Trying To Control Others

The goal is power and control. The means are anger and violence.

Violence isn't always about going nuts. Sure, I often hear, "Ron I don't know what happened, I just lost it." But much more often I hear, "I didn't get what I wanted so I got mad" statements. Jenny's case is a good example.

Jenny is a mother of three who has trouble with anger. She used to be much worse, though. Before, she raged. Now she "spanks" her kids "whenever they need a good paddling." And when is that? You guessed it. Whenever they don't do what she wants, which is all the time. Why, just yesterday Barry came home with a mohawk haircut. Terrible. And Suzanne keeps hassling her about wanting to date. Sometimes Jenny wonders why she has such awful kids.

Jenny thinks she's a lot better. She says she can stay in control of her anger now. All she does is spank, "and I stop before I lose control."

Meanwhile, her kids ignore her until she starts getting violent. They're out of control. They don't obey. Last week they stole money from her room. And nine-year-old Timothy gets sent home from school for fighting every few days.

What to do? "Guess I'll have to spank them some more. Until they learn I'm in charge."

No, Jenny, wake up! It's not working. It's not going to work. You don't need to spank more. You need to spank less. Mostly, you need to let go of the need to control everything your children do.

Jenny, forget about Barry's haircut. It's his head, not yours. Sit down and talk with Suzanne about safe dating practices. She's sixteen and she's going to see boys whether you like it or not. You can't stop her, not even with violence.

You're raging because you think others owe you. They should give you everything you want. Well, they won't. They're not on this planet just to serve you. They've got lives of their own. They owe you nothing. So quit trying to make them pay.

Face reality. You can't control the world. Give up the wish to be king or queen. You're not God, either, so please put down the lightning bolts before you get burned.

Stop Chasing and Holding

Spend the rent money on a trip to the casino? Seems like a great idea to you. Unfortunately, Karen doesn't agree the first time you suggest it. So you say it again. She still doesn't agree, right? So you follow her into the living room "just to make your point." And into the kitchen. Hell, you won't even let her go to the bathroom without you. Talking. Arguing. Trying to convince her. Trying to wear her down.

Angry people have Velcro minds. Everything sticks. You can't let go of an idea, no matter how ridiculous. Difference isn't allowed, either. Everybody else has to think just like you. If they don't, chase after them until they do.

"But, Ron, she has to agree with me. It's so important. I can't stop until she tells me I'm right." Bull.

Rule Four To Control Your Anger:
Accept Difference

People think and act differently than you. Let them. Quit chasing after them. Quit holding them down until they "understand." They have a right to their own opinions. So do you.

I want to repeat something I said in Chapter 4. Holding and chasing are two forms of violence. They take away the rights to privacy and freedom of movement. You must learn to *say what you have to say once and only once*. Then sit down. Stay quiet. People listen a lot better when you're not hassling them.

No More Demands and Threats

Sharon is livid. She told LeRoy to buy roses for her birthday. He took her to dinner instead. What a moron! "LeRoy, you're gonna buy me roses. Do it now or else."

Do it or else. Demand and threaten. The traditional angry communication style—rude and crude bully stuff.

Some angry people act like they have got a gun that will never run out of ammunition. Bam! Bam! Bam! Shoot them all down. If they stand up, shoot them again. Do it or else. Do it or else. Do it or else. But all guns eventually run out of ammo. By now LeRoy's sick of Sharon's demands and threats. She better change her ways or find a new guy.

Demands and threats wear out. They may work for a while. You may get what you want right now. But that soon changes. The people you've pushed around get resentful. They sneer in your face if they're strong enough, or behind your back if they're not. They laugh at you.

I counseled a grown-up bully named Jeff. He was always throwing his weight around. He demanded the best office and the newest equipment. He'd complain for weeks if he didn't get it. The more he received, the more he wanted. But it wasn't working. Instead of the newest, Jeff was getting the oldest equipment. He got the slowest service, too. The more special treatment he demanded, the worse things got.

Jeff made enemies of his co-workers. His demands turned them off. He needed a new strategy. Together we came up with one that began with the next two rules for climbing down the ladder.

Rule Five To Control Your Anger: Ask, Don't Demand

It's simple enough when you admit you have no claim on other people's time, money, bodies, and souls. Until then, it's tough.

I'm not talking about just saying "please" and "thank you." That helps, but it may be phony. "Please do it my way (or I'll kill you)" is still a demand.

We have a family rule. Never ask a yes-or-no question unless you can accept either answer. That's what I mean by ask, don't demand.

Let's use sex for an example. You're hot. You really want to make love. So ask. "Honey, how about tonight? Interested?" Good luck and happy seduction.

But what if the answer is "No, not tonight." She's tired. Or he's just not feeling sexy. Now what? Well, you could try whining, crying, moping, or nagging. "Oh, honey, come on. Just once. Just this time. I promise not to pester you again. Please. Please. I know I said I wouldn't do this, but how about it. Let's go to bed right now," and so on, and so on.

You could try demanding. "Hey, I'm your spouse. I have rights. I want sex, so give it to me." I want, I want, I want.

Or you could *accept* your partner's choice. He or she said no. No means no. Period. Who said you'd get laid whenever you wanted? Nobody, because that's not reality. Instead of demanding, accept that no tonight. And that doesn't mean turning away and not saying good night, either. Be decent. It's not the end of the world.

Ask, don't demand. Be grateful if you get what you ask for. Be polite if you don't.

Rule Six To Control Your Anger: Reward, Don't Punish or Threaten

"Do it or else" usually means "or else I'll do something nasty to you." It means punishment and the threat of punishment. Do what I want so you don't get hurt.

Angry people don't know much about rewards. They're better at punishments. That's what they got as kids. It's hard to give what you never got.

So what? You can't go on like this forever. Maybe the threats and punishments scare the crap out of the people you love. But that's it.

Reward, don't punish or threaten. Let's go back to the bedroom. Last night you accepted a no. Tonight your partner says yes. You have a great time together. You're both satisfied. And then you hear this. "Honey, you've changed. Now when we have sex I feel loved, not just used. I really like it when you are nice to me."

How about that? Make love, not war. Act decent and people feel good around you.

Some rewards you can give are material: money, letting your kid drive the car, a candy bar. The most important ones, though, are your words. Praise. Thoughtful comments. Understanding. Listening. We'll spend more time on this in the next chapter (the no more blaming and shaming section). For now, just think about what you can say and do to reward instead of punish.

Summary

It's hard work to climb down the anger and violence ladder. The first six rules that we've looked at in this chapter will help.

1. Take a time-out to stop the violence.

2. Wipe that frown off your face and relax.

3. Quit trying to control others.

4. Accept difference.

5. Ask, don't demand.

6. Reward, don't punish or threaten.

Let's continue now, to the bottom half of the ladder. You're about half way to a decent life, so don't quit now.

7

Climbing Down the Ladder, Part 2— Keep That Foul Mouth Shut Until You Learn To Talk Right

> Ron, it's not violence. Buddy never hits me. It's his mouth. The names he calls me. When Buddy gets mad he'll say anything to hurt me. And he yells as loud as he can. I feel better when he's gone than when he's home. I don't know how much longer I can stand this.

Betty is married to an angry talker. True, Buddy's not physically dangerous. Long ago he learned not to hit. But he still has a big anger problem. He gets mad a lot, and then he attacks with words. He yells and screams. He swears at her. He calls her terrible names. He criticizes. He looks for her faults and tells everyone about them. He blames and shames.

I guess it works. Betty does feel awful after one of these scenes. Those nasty words hurt her worse than any blows. Another victory for Buddy. Another marriage being ruined.

You know what Buddy's biggest complaint is? That Betty seems cold and distant. That she doesn't trust him. I wonder why?

Buddy says he has the right to say anything he wants. That's true. He can swear, shout, and name-call as much as he wants. It's mostly legal. But face facts. This is low-level communication. You're in bad shape if your best sentence looks like a line from a comic book (##*****!!\\\#######!). It's not something to be proud of. You might as well carry a sign that says you have an anger problem.

Climbing Down the Last Four Steps

We're going down the last four rungs on the anger and violence ladder. That means stopping shouting, screaming, and swearing. No more blaming and shaming, either. The cold shoulder game must end. And let's get rid of sneaky anger while we're at it.

Rule Seven To Control Your Anger: Speak Quietly and Don't Swear

> Hey, Ron, now just hold on a minute. I need to shout and swear. It's good for me. That's how I let off steam. I'll go nuts if I have to be nice all the time.

Sorry, but I mean it. No swearing, shouting, or screaming. Not even if others shout or swear at you. Speak quietly and don't swear. Remember, you've had trouble with anger all your life. You've said more than your share of nasty things already. You've screwed up your life big time, and mostly with your mouth. Once you get started you won't stop. You'll go on and on. One good cuss leads to another, doesn't it? Swearing, shouting, and screaming are like potato chips. You'll never stop after only one.

I know these are some of your favorite weapons. You can really zap people with your loud mouth. You're good at it. It's easy to hurt others that way, especially your family and closest friends.

So here's the trade-off:

Quit swearing, shouting, and screaming (and the blaming and sham-ing we'll soon discuss) and you'll get more of what you want.

You will get more of what you want when you learn how to talk decently. When you speak to others with respect, you'll get treated a whole lot better.

A habitually angry person is like a kid carrying a handful of pennies. Offer the kid a ten dollar bill for the pennies. He'll refuse. Those pennies seem so valuable.

Your anger is small change. You'll have to put it down to pick up the real money.

Warning: Don't expect instant results. The first few times you speak quietly people might not notice. They may not change what they say or do right away. But they will. Treat them decently and you'll eventually get treated well yourself.

Replace Blaming and Shaming with Responsibility and Respect

"You did it. You made me do it. It's all your fault." This kind of blaming is a disaster for angry people. Why? Because you'll never change if you blame others for your actions.

Rule Eight To Control Your Anger: Be Responsible for Everything You Say and Do

Nobody else is responsible. Forget the phrase "you make me mad." It's worthless. "I'm making myself angry" is a lot more honest.

So who have you been blaming for your anger and misery? Your partner? Your parents? Your boss? "Them?" God? It's time to let go of these excuses. They aren't the cause of your unhappiness anymore. You are.

You can recover from your anger, and you will. But only if you accept complete responsibility for your words and deeds.

You are the owner of your mouth. You are responsible for everything that comes out of it.

Rule Nine To Control Your Anger: Treat Others with Respect

Treating people with respect breaks down to a list of do's and don'ts.

Treating Others With Respect

Do:

begin each day with a promise to respect others

sit down and talk quietly

listen carefully to what others say

look for things to appreciate in others

give praise out loud for the good you see in others

tell others they are good, good enough, and lovable

tell them they are worthwhile and important

speak in a quiet voice even when you disagree

pass up chances to insult, attack, or criticize

let others have responsibility for their lives while you take responsibility for yours

Don't:

look for things to criticize

make fun of or laugh at others

make faces or roll your eyes

tell people how to run their lives

insult

ignore

put people down in front of others

act superior

sneer

tell people they're weird or crazy

say they are bad, not good enough, or unlovable

say they don't belong or you wish they were dead

call them names like fat, ugly, stupid, or worthless

None of this is easy. You have a habit of blaming and shaming. It will take a firm promise to yourself to speak and act with respect. But it's worth it. Treat others fairly and you'll be treated fairly.

Here's how to start. Go back to the list of don'ts. Circle all the ones you're doing even once in a while. Put a star by the ones you do a lot. Then decide which one or two you can change right now. Not the whole list, just one or two. Remember, you've got the rest of your life to get better.

No bullshit, please. No "I'll *try* to quit criticizing, or sneering, or name-calling." You've been trying enough. Very trying. This is the time for *doing*! If your goal is to stop name-calling, that means 100 percent stopping, not most of the time.

Look, you've been drinking poison every day—anger poison. Is it really any better to drink it every other day? Of course not. It's time to throw away the bottle.

Take a good look at the list of do's. Pick one or two. Practice them. If it's praising others, don't let the words get stuck in your throat. "Well, I thought he was nice, but I didn't tell him." Why not? Were you afraid your mouth would fall off from shock? Come on! Now is the moment to change. Now is the only moment. Change never happens tomorrow.

When Silence Isn't Golden

We talked in earlier chapters about the cold shoulder, the weapon of silence. Taking the phone off the hook and leaving it off. "I'm mad at you, so I won't say anything." Disconnection.

I've seen a lot of angry people get stuck on this rung of the ladder. They don't hit anymore. They don't threaten. They don't curse. They don't criticize.

They do pout. They sulk. They watch TV for hours. They take silent walks—long silent walks that don't help. They get moody and sullen. When someone asks them what's wrong they usually say "Nothing," or "If you don't know by now I'm not gonna say," or "I just need some time alone."

They aren't taking a time-out. A time-out is to calm down so that you can talk. This is different. It's a direct use of anger. The goal is to hurt someone, to punish. The weapon is silence. Silence tells others they aren't even worth talking to.

Most anger is hot. But not this kind. This is *cold* anger. Frozen. It can easily turn into resentment and hate. The main problem with it is that *nothing gets solved through silence.*

*Rule Ten To Control Your Anger: Tell Others What
Bothers You. Be Direct, Specific, and Polite*

Be direct. No more cold shoulders. No lectures, either.
Just tell the truth. "Honey, I'm angry because you said you'd
be home at ten o'clock and now it's midnight." That's it. No
need for hours of angry silence. Save the "if you loved me
. . . " lecture. They've heard it all before.

Be specific. Don't be vague. "Sue, I kinda, sorta want
you to, you know, be nicer to me." Excuse me, but you have
just said nothing at all. Compare that with, "Sue, please turn
off the TV when you talk with me on the phone." Sue may
not like your request, of course. But at least she knows what
you want. You're being specific and honest.

Be polite. Polite means "showing good manners toward
others." Polite people are courteous and tactful—the opposite
of rude and crude. You can be polite even when you are angry.
That's what normal people do. They get angry *and* they stay
polite. Amazing, isn't it?

The Last Rung—No More Sneaky Anger

Forgetting half on purpose. Leaving things out. Whining and
complaining. Playing dumb. "Yeah, but." These are examples
of sneaky anger. Frustrating others while never admitting you
are angry.

Angry people don't usually think of themselves as
sneaky—not about their anger. They think it's pretty darn
obvious when they get mad. Often they're right.

However, sometimes they do also practice sneaky anger.
They may be sneaky with people in power ("I hate that dumb
SOB boss. I have to follow orders. But I'll go real slow."). Or
when they're trying to look good ("I thought Bets never got
mad about anything when we started dating. But she's sure
different now.").

Angry people often get sneaky after they've done something bad with their anger. That's when they vow never to
get angry again. They try too hard. "I just won't get mad, no

matter what. I'll get along with everybody. I'll never get angry again." Guilt, guilt, guilt. They hide their anger from others. They hide it from themselves.

Rule Eleven To Control Your Anger: Use "I" Statements

No two people agree on everything. Conflict is certain. You can fight about money, the kids, power and control, religion, anything and everything. The trick is to disagree without killing each other.

You've already seen the do's and don'ts of respect. Now let's add a simple communication device that helps keep talk direct, specific, and polite. It's called using *"I" statements*. These have been around a long time for one reason. They work.

An "I" statement has three parts:

1. Some *specific action* that bothers you.
   "Henry, you spent the rent money on tapes and CD's."

2. Your *feelings*.
   "And now I feel angry and scared."

3. Your *wants*.
   "I want you to take that stuff back right now, before you open it."

Henry blew it. He's wasted precious rent money on his favorite rock group. Joan is upset, with reason. But Joan's dealing with her anger problem. She can't afford to get furious. Besides, she doesn't want to give Henry a chance to get off the hook. He'll make her anger the problem if she goes nuts.

Enter the "I" statement. It's just three sentences, with no swearing, no put-downs, no eyeball-popping rages, no high blood pressure. Just the facts.

Maybe Henry will still act like a moron. But if so, he'll be the only one.

Sneaky anger never works well. It's like driving a car with one foot on the brake. Better to learn how to tell people what's bothering you. You'll get where you want to go a lot faster that way.

Summary

Climbing down the anger and violence ladder takes time and effort. First you have to control your fists, and then your mouth.

We've added five new rules to the first batch. Let's list all eleven now:

1. Take a time-out to stop the violence.

2. Wipe that frown off your face and relax.

3. Quit trying to control others.

4. Accept difference.

5. Ask, don't demand.

6. Reward, don't punish or threaten.

7. Speak quietly and don't swear.

8. Be responsible for what you say and do.

9. Treat others with respect.

10. Tell others what bothers you. Be direct, specific, and polite.

11. Use "I" statements.

Nothing very complicated here. Eleven simple rules. Follow them and you'll have a better life. Ignore them and stay miserable.

Onward now, toward two chapters on special problems. The first is the belief that others are deliberately trying to mess you up. (As if you needed help!) The second is how anger turns into resentment and hate.

8

Believe It or Not, They're Not Out To Get You

Severly angry people think funny thoughts—not ha-ha funny, strange funny. And that's certainly nothing to laugh about.

"Everyone's out to get me."

"You can't trust anyone."

"I have to defend myself all the time."

"They're all jealous of me."

"I'm good and they're bad."

"They just want to use me."

"The world's a totally dangerous place."

"They're plotting against me."

Angry people have negative thoughts and angry, hostile ideas. They live in a mean, dog-eat-dog world—a world in which others sit around all day thinking of ways to make them miserable.

Paranoia is the belief that others are out to get you. "Others" could be total strangers, the FBI, the folks at work, your partner, your kids, everybody. Sure they say they love you, but so what? You know better. Beneath that smile is a frown waiting for you when you turn around. They're probably talking about you right now. Saying nasty things and plotting ways to harm you.

Think I'm exaggerating? Well, I am, a little. But not much. Most habitually angry people believe the world's a pretty bad place. Why? Because they think others are as angry as they are.

Here's the angry person's chain of bad thinking:

1. I'm mad at them, so they must be mad at me.

2. No matter how friendly they seem, don't trust them.

3. Look for proof they are trying to hurt me.

4. Get ready to defend myself.

5. The best defense is a good offense, so attack first.

The first sentence is the big one. It starts the ball rolling. Remember that angry people are mad, mad, mad. They wake up mad. They stay mad. They go to bed mad. They assume that everybody is like they are.

> Others must be like me. They must be angry all the time, because I am. Oh sure, others don't seem angry. They cover it up, but deep down they must be pissed.

Angry people "give away" their anger to others (the technical name for this is *projection*). But they still have plenty left over. They may run out of sugar, or money, or hope, but they always keep a supply of anger.

Overly angry people have little trust. Trust means we can rely on people. Others won't deliberately hurt us. We have confidence in them. We're on the same side. We aren't enemies. But angry people need enemies so they can stay mad.

Angry people create problems. They do that to have something to fight about. *They also create enemies.* After all, an enemy is someone you can always be angry at. The more enemies, the more you can excuse your anger.

Angry people constantly look for reasons to be angry. Remember those anger invitations I mentioned in earlier chapters? An anger invitation is anything we could use as an excuse to get mad. Things like the neighbors' dogs barking, children fighting, wanting to buy a hundred dollar coat with twelve dollars in your pocket. In the introduction, I wrote that angry people say "yes, thanks" to far too many anger invitations. Well, they do more than that. *They write their own invitations.* Then they sign somebody else's name and mail them to themselves.

Here's an example. Jake's boss Melva tells him she's been watching his work. She likes what she sees. He's up for a promotion soon and she'll support him. Pretty good deal? Not to Jake.

> What an insult! How dare she keep an eye on me. Melva has no right to judge me. Who does she think she is?

Jake's turned a compliment into an insult. He's written his own anger invitation and forged Melva's name.

Here's another situation. Helene's boyfriend Chad tells her he's falling in love with her. Maybe she smiles, but inside she thinks:

> Men. They only want one thing. He's just saying this to get me into bed.

She feels used and abused. That evening she picks a fight with Chad and breaks up with him. Helene's made Chad into an enemy. She's sure he wrote the anger invitation, of course. But we know better. We saw her think it, write it, sign his name, and mail it to herself.

Angry people look for proof that others are trying to hurt them. It's easy to find proof—too easy. Here's why.

Bad messages - - - **Neutral messages** - - - Good messages

Most messages we get are neutral. They're neither good nor bad. They're mostly about facts. Pass the potatoes. It's raining outside. Please set the alarm clock.

A few messages are negative. I'm mad at you. You're a jerk. Get lost. Go play in traffic.

A few are positive. I love you. You're OK. I like that shirt you're wearing. Come closer.

Angry people turn neutral messages into bad ones. "Pass the potatoes" must mean you think I'll eat them all. "It's raining outside?" Of course it's raining, I can see that. Do you think I'm stupid? "Please set the alarm." Why? Do you think I'm lazy or something?

Angry people even turn good messages into bad ones. She's always saying "I love you." Why? Maybe she's messing around and feeling guilty. "You're OK." Huh, they don't mean that. They really think I stink. She likes that shirt I'm wearing, does she? Well, it's none of her business what I wear or don't wear. "Come closer." Why? So you can kick me? No way.

See what I mean? Angry people create enemies. They make the world into an ugly, nasty, dangerous place. They turn gold into lead.

"They're out to get me," thinks the angry person.

I need to defend myself. Better get ready. Be suspicious. Don't trust anybody. Look for secret plans and hidden agendas. Prepare to fight. Prepare to flee.

Prepare to attack. See, I know you're gonna hurt me, even though you say you won't. Why should I just wait around? Better to go after you first. Get the first blow in. Nail you before you nail me.

That's why Bill called Mary a slut the other day. Because she put him down. Or she would if he let her. That's why Hannah walked off the job, too. Before her boss could fire her. And that's why Dan got so mad at Norene when she said she loved him. Dan won't let anybody get close enough to hurt him.

Paranoia is a way of thinking; a way of living. Defensive. Suspicious. Doubtful. Angry. Hostile. Mean. Get them or they'll get you. Don't trust anybody.

Believe it or not, they're not out to get you.

It's that simple. No, people don't spend hours every day thinking of ways to harm you. They've got better things to do with their lives.

I'm not asking you to be a blind optimist. You don't have to become a sucker to let go of your rage. But you do need to think differently. Here's how.

Rules for Rational Thinking

Do
challenge old thoughts
    that keep you angry
think anti-anger
    thoughts.

Don't
awfulize
devilize

How To Think Better

Albert Ellis, the founder of rational-emotive therapy, talks a lot about irrational thinking—funny thinking. You are thinking funny when you create enemies or problems. There are a lot of ways to think irrationally, but I'm only going to write about two. These two are very common among those who get angry a lot. Change them and you'll change your life.

Don't Awfulize

We *awfulize* by deciding that something hideous is happening to us. It's horrible, terrible, dreadful. It's a catastrophe, unbearable. We have to do something. We have to get mad.

If problems were like rain, habitually angry people would never have gentle sprinkles. Nor occasional showers. Not even thunderstorms. Only hurricanes.

Angry people turn disappointments into disasters. They're wonderful at awfulizing.

Cassie wants to go to the country-western festival this weekend, but she is scheduled to work on Saturday. Unfortunately, she can't find anybody to trade days. "This is terrible," she thinks. "If I don't go I'll be miserable." She doesn't and she is. So she takes out her frustration on her friends and co-workers.

Stanley asks Shirley out, but she's busy. "Call me tomorrow evening," she says. But not Stan. By then he'll be stirring his anger like a straw through a strong drink. "I hate rejection," Stan wails. He feels crushed. And defeated. And very, very angry.

Awfulizing keeps the fires burning. But you can douse the flames. Just ask yourself two questions:

- If this were the last day of my life, how much would this really matter?

- Compared with my worst disappointment ever, where does this one rank?

Most of the time you'll see that your disappointment is pretty small. It's nothing to sue God about; no reason to scream, hit, or stay angry forever.

The phrase "It's no big deal" helps a lot. It keeps you from turning disappointments into disasters. It keeps you from awfulizing.

Don't Devilize

Eggs aren't deviled until we make them that way. It's the same with people. They don't become devils unless we make them into devils. The recipe looks like this:

One dash(ed) hope that someone will do exactly what you want

One cup of frustration

One pound of leftover resentments (see the next chapter to learn how to make these really tough)

A teaspoon of bitters

Pour on concentrated anger and mix these ingredients. Sift in an ounce of suspicion that he or
she is doing something to you on purpose. Neatly
divide the world into good and bad parts. Place
yourself on the good side. Put the mixture on the
bad side. Make sure it stays there forever. Throw the
whole thing in the oven until it is half-baked.

Take from oven. Wrinkle your nose at the bad
smell. Decorate it with horns. Now you can call the
person you're mad at a devil.

Devilizing means believing that somebody is evil. Darth
Vader evil. Satan evil. Totally bad. Meanwhile, you get to be
perfect, pure, and innocent. You're completely good. They're
lower than pond scum.

Why do people devilize? Because that gives them another
reason to be angry and violent. The thinking goes like this:

If I'm good and you're bad, then I have the right to
destroy you. I get to squash you like a bug, and I
don't have to feel guilty.

For instance: Millie fails an important test. Now she can't
get into that advanced library science class. She could admit
she partied instead of studied, but she's got a better reason.

It's my teacher. She's terrible. Nobody learns anything. Besides, she hates me because I'm smarter
than her. She's a horrible person. They should fire
her.

Sure. Better heat up the oven, because Millie is cooking up
another devil.

Another example: Ulysses is terribly envious of his brother
Hector's hunting skills. Hector can search, shoot, and snare
better than Ulysses. Ulysses could try to learn from his brother,
of course. But that's not his style. Instead, he makes up a
story that Hector is really tagging other hunters' deer. Ulysses
tries to get everybody mad at Hector. Worse, he begins to
believe his own lies. Soon he won't go hunting with Hector

anymore. Hector is the devil. Ulysses has become an innocent victim in his own eyes.

Devilizing must stop. You can't recover from anger problems and still devilize. Instead, keep these thoughts in mind:

- Good people can and do disagree.

- Just because someone disagrees with you doesn't make them bad.

- We don't live in a black-and-white world.

Challenge Old Thoughts That Keep You Angry

There are four kinds of thoughts that help keep people angry:

- Rigid beliefs about the world

- Rigid beliefs about yourself

- Thinking you're helpless

- Blaming others for your anger

Rigid Beliefs About the World
"You can't trust anybody."
"Never believe a man/woman."
"It's a cruel world. You have to fight to stay alive."
I've already talked about these beliefs based on paranoia. Hang onto them and you'll stay angry and alone.

The counter-thought: "The world is neither good nor bad. It just is."

Rigid Beliefs About Yourself
"I'm just an angry person and I always will be."
"Anger runs in my family. That's why I'm angry."
"I'm a born fighter."
"I'm a man and men are naturally aggressive."
"I'm Irish/Italian/a redhead (and you know how angry we get)."

You're excusing your anger by saying it's a natural part of you; a matter of genetics; part of your gender, family, or nationality.

What a crock! Sure, there are a lot of angry men out there, but most of them are a lot less angry than you. The same with redheads, Italians, and all the rest. And look at your family again. You'll find that some members of your family are calm. People are not born fighters. Besides, you're old enough to take charge of your own life.

The counter-thought: "No matter what my background, I am responsible for my current actions."

Thinking You're Helpless

"My anger takes over. I can't stop it."

"It's my drinking. That's when I lose control. I can't stop."

"PMS. That's the problem. It's not my fault. It's my body."

I hear a lot of these excuses. Yes, you have a problem. Physical, emotional, or mental. But you *can* stop your anger. You *can* get angry less often. You *can* let go of your anger quicker. You *can* be angry and stay respectful. It takes planning, and courage, and skill.

The counter-thought: "I'll make no excuses. I can and will control my anger."

Blaming Others for Your Anger

"I'm a victim of abuse. It's their fault. I can't change."

"It's all her fault. She made me mad."

"Living with an alcoholic would make anybody into a witch."

You may have been beaten, raped, abused, misused, or neglected in the past. Some of you grew up in terribly angry families (see Chapter 3).

Big deal. The past is over. The pain is done. Think: How many years have gone by? How often have you used your past as an excuse? As a cheap way to hurt people? Now is the time to let go of that excuse.

The counter-thought: "The past is dead. I won't use it to excuse my anger anymore. I will live in the present."

Think Anti-Anger Thoughts

Don't let yourself be controlled by angry thoughts. Instead, follow this sequence:

- Catch your angry thought.
- Stop it.
- Think an anti-anger thought.

Does this sound easy? Well, it is easy, with practice.

First, watch for angry thoughts like those described at the beginning of the chapter. Watch for times when you awfulize or devilize, blame your past, or anything else you use as an excuse to get mad. Then challenge those thoughts. Don't let them run your life. Then start thinking in better ways.

Here are some examples of the anti-anger sequence.

Tim's wife Judy asks him to take the kids for a walk.

> *Old thought:* She has no right to tell me what to do.
>
> *Old result:* A fight.
>
> *Challenge:* Tim, here you go again. Stop before you get angry.
>
> *New thought:* Judy's just asking. I can say yes or no. She's not trying to boss me around.

Betty Ann is told by her probation officer to report to her office.

> *Old thought:* %#@*&^%$%#.
>
> *Old result:* Betty's enraged before she even sees the probation officer.
>
> *Challenge:* Whoa, slow down.
>
> *New thought:* Take it easy. Wait until you find out what's going on.

Benny's girlfriend Chrissy talks with a guy.

> *Old thought:* He's gonna try to get in her jeans. Time for a battle.

Old result: Benny makes a fool of himself.

Challenge: Stop! Don't be an idiot.

New thought: "I'll trust Chrissy. She's a big girl and she can take care of herself."

See the pattern? First, you catch yourself thinking some old thought that triggers your anger. Next, you slow everything down by challenging that thought. Then you replace that anger-increasing idea with an anti-anger thought.

You may need help with this from friends, partners, or counselors. It might be hard to recognize the thoughts that get you angry. But you can do it, and it will help a lot.

Thought stopping is the hardest part of changing your thinking habits. Those old thoughts are like wagons stuck in a deep rut. You hear yourself thinking them over and over. They drive you crazy. And others give you that "Oh, God, there he goes again" look.

Thought stopping happens when you insist to yourself you won't let those old thoughts run your life anymore. It's usually a slow process, though. Here's what you can do to help get rid of the old thoughts.

First, tell yourself you're sick and tired of a thought that makes you angry. "Every time I think Sally is screwing around on me we get into a huge fight. I hate my jealousy and I'm going to do something about it now."

Next, count how often you think that thought. Keep score. Get a little notebook and make a mark each time that thought pops into your head. "101 . . . 102 . . . 103. And it's only three o'clock. I'm in big trouble here." Just count. Don't even try to change things yet.

Then, set a goal. The idea is to catch yourself as soon as you have the thought, before it has a chance to grab and hold you. "All right. As soon as I start getting jealous I'll tell myself to *stop right now*." Remember you'll need a substitute thought to fill the void. "I'll stop and tell myself I can trust Sally and I love her."

Don't expect 100 percent success. But reward yourself every time you succeed. Give yourself a little praise. "Yes, I did it. I stopped myself from being jealous just now. That's the fourth time today. I'm getting there." Notice the good feelings. The relief. The feeling of being free.

Don't beat yourself up when you fail. The goal is to slowly get rid of that old thought. Just laugh a little about it when you finally realize it got you again. "Uh-oh. I just spent another fifteen minutes getting jealous. That's about forty-five minutes today . . . times seven for this week makes over five hours . . . times fifty-two weeks in a year . . . times ten years . . . Am I having fun yet?"

Thought stopping takes time. Mostly you must really want to change. You can alter your thoughts. It's your choice.

Summary

People stay angry because of their thoughts. We've looked at quite a few of these thoughts in this chapter. The main point is to think differently. Quit blaming others for your anger, pain, and past. Take responsibility for your anger. Let go of paranoia. Trust the world a little more.

There is still one major problem: resentments. Angry people are masters at making and keeping them. That's the topic of the next chapter.

9

Saying Good-bye to Old Resentments

Jeff had an affair. Mary Lou found out. He broke it off, apologized, vowed he'd never do it again. And he's kept his word for four years. But Mary Lou won't forgive him. She won't forget. She says she's tried to, but can't. Mary Lou brings up the affair about once a week. But she thinks about it constantly. She checks on Jeff's movements. She tells her friends and family that he's a terrible husband. She criticizes him about everything, about nothing. Their sex life is awful. She can't imagine why she stays married. Mary Lou hates Jeff for what he did to her.

What does it mean to hate? First, hate is a *dislike* of somebody or something. But that's not enough, is it? You may detest banana pudding, but you probably won't lose sleep over it. No, dislike itself isn't enough.

Hate starts out as anger. To get to hate, you have to add some more ingredients:

- *Strength.* Hatred is strong. You don't hate somebody a little.

- *Great emotion.* The person who hates is dealing with an emotion as powerful and demanding as love.

- *Threat.* The person we hate seems to be a major threat to our lives, our values, or to what we own. He or she is bad because of this threat.

- *Time.* Hate builds up over time. Sometimes it develops slowly, sometimes fast. Once built, though, it lasts. Sometimes it sticks around a lifetime.

- *Inability to let go.* Hate hangs around like a boring dinner guest. It's awfully hard to let go of hate, even when you want to.

- *Desire for revenge.* People who hate feel wounded. They often want to hurt others as much as they have been hurt.

- *Interference with normal life.* Hatred takes up a lot of energy. You can't think of anything else. You do things that don't make sense. You are driven by your hate. The person you hate haunts you. Hate is a wolf howling in your mind.

Hate begins as anger. You feel upset about something. You blame somebody for causing that problem. The problem doesn't get solved. Then you get more angry. You can't stop thinking about it. You begin to resent the other person. You dwell on what he did to you. The injuries feel unforgivable. The resentment turns into hate, like slowly hardening concrete. Your attitude toward the other person becomes rigid. Nothing he says or does makes any difference. He is bad and you are good. It's that simple.

Unfortunately, resentment comes easy to those who are very angry. Too easy. Hate provides a perfect excuse to stay angry. You can hate somebody forever, even after they're dead. You can always blame them for your problems, too.

> You bet I'm angry. After all she did to me, of course I'm furious. I'll never forget her, you know. I'll stay mad at my mother till the day I die.

Melvin means it, too. Never mind the damage he's doing to

himself. Who cares about the rest of the family? He hates that woman. That's all that's important.

Others may struggle to let go of their hate. They can see that their resentments are hurting them more than anyone else. But it's not an easy job.

Hatreds are like deeply rooted weeds. They don't pull up easily. And, like weeds, they sprout quickly and grow fast, even if you try to ignore them. Left alone, hate crowds out other feelings. Love is one of them; it gets choked out by the weeds of resentment and hate.

Hate hurts you more than anybody else.

Hate can take over your life; it destroys your peace of mind. It keeps you stuck in the past, nursing old wounds. You can't get on with your life. You can't grow or change. *Hate is a luxury you can't afford.*

Of course, you can keep your resentments and hatreds. Nobody can make you give them up. But you'll pay a big price. Resentment is expensive. Here's the bill.

- You can't get the person you hate out of your mind (what AA members call letting someone have free rent in your brain).

- You think so much about what you hate that it's hard to do anything you could enjoy.

- You feel frustrated and angry much of the time. You become upset more often and stay mad longer.

- You feel sorry for yourself and how you've suffered, but you don't think you can do anything about it.

- You get irritable with others, and your relationships suffer.

- You see others as bad or thoughtless people out to hurt you.

- You may say or do things that you later regret or that get you in trouble.

- You may become bitter and depressed.

Preventive Gardening

It's easy to control weeds. Just pull them up while they are small. I'll write soon about how to get rid of full-grown hatreds. But the best thing is not to let them grow at all. Practice preventive gardening.

Direct, honest talk is the world's best weed puller. That means using the rules listed in Chapters 6 and 7. Some of the most important ones are to use "I" statements, treat others with respect, and to tell others what bothers you.

Charlie feels hurt and angry. His best friend at work just "stole" a customer Charlie had been handling. Charlie did the work but Mike got the sale.

"OK," says Charlie. "I'll try what Ron suggests. I'll talk with Mike right now." And he does. Mike listens, realizes he was wrong, and apologizes. He even offers to turn the commission over to Charlie. Instead, they split it.

Charlie still has to do one thing, though. He needs to *let go* of his hurt and anger. Really be done with it. He reminds himself they are good friends. He remembers they've worked together for years. He forgives Mike. He drops the subject.

Direct talk works most of the time. Treat people decently and you'll get what you want. But what if you don't?

Same situation. But this time Mike gets defensive. "Go to hell, Charlie," he says. "I made the sale. They were my customers. Butt out."

Now what?

Remember, you are in charge. *Only you have the power to stop a resentment from growing.*

Let's look at Charlie's choices. He could:

- Get real nasty
- Forget the whole thing
- Repeat his complaint but stay calm
- Try to get help from his boss
- Stay mad for weeks

- Drop it for now but come back later
- Quit his job
- Vow to get even

Which of these choices would build resentments? Four of them: Vowing to get even, staying mad for weeks, getting real nasty, and quitting.

Which would least build resentments? Repeating his complaint calmly, dropping it for a little while but coming back to it soon, and asking for help.

What about forgetting the whole thing? That could go either way. Forgetting it might work if Charlie can tell himself it's no big deal. Maybe Mike was just being a good salesman in a very competitive job. Maybe Charlie would have done exactly the same. If so, drop it. But forgetting about it might be a mistake. Sometimes you do have to speak up. Be honest with yourself here. Can you let it go? If you drop it, will it happen again and again? Could any good come out of saying something again?

This world's not always fair or kind. Bad things do happen to good people. Do what you can to make things right. But be careful. You can't fix the world. Don't let everything that goes wrong turn into a resentment.

Here are some do's and don't that help keep resentments from building:

Preventing Resentful Feelings

Do	Don't
stick to the issue	turn a disappointment into a disaster
ask yourself what the problem is and what you can do to help	let yourself think, act, or feel like a victim
throw away old scorecards; concentrate on today	dwell on what the other person is doing to you
get help if you need it	go back to old games
be responsible for your own happiness	judge the whole person because of one thing you dislike

Forgiving

Ed was badly hurt by his girlfriend Lee. She let him get close. Then she ran away. Lee played emotional hide-and-seek with Ed for years. Then she dumped him.

Ed didn't let go easily. He cursed her daily. He bad-mouthed her to others. He sent her nasty letters. He turned her in for child neglect just to hurt her. Then one morning he woke up in a sweat. Once again he'd dreamt about killing her. "This is enough," he said. Ed needed to do something to quit hating.

What do you do about the fully grown weeds in your garden—the resentments and hatreds that have been around for years? Like Ed, you'll need a special garden tool to get rid of them. That tool is forgiving.

Forgiving has two special definitions. First, *to forgive means to drop your resentments*. Second, *to forgive means giving up any claims on the other person*. They don't owe you anything anymore. Not money. Not an apology. Not love.

You quit being a victim when you forgive. You take back control of your life. The good things in your garden have space to grow.

Forgiving is a powerful choice for anybody. It's vital for rageaholics. *You will never quit raging until you learn to forgive.* Period. That's the bottom line. Hang onto your hate if you like. Grow those weeds. Put a ton of fertilizer on them. Stay bitter and mean-spirited. *Or* learn to forgive. Let go. Give yourself a chance at a new life.

There are several important things to know about forgiving.

Forgiving is a choice. You don't have to forgive anyone. And you don't have to forgive another until you are ready, even if that person apologizes or tries to make amends. Forgiving someone has to be a voluntary choice. It's not something to do because you "should" forgive or because someone tells you to.

Maybe you're not able to forgive yet. Perhaps the pain is too fresh. You don't have to hurry.

But don't wait forever. Don't look for excuses to put it off. The weeds get bigger every day. Ask yourself these questions if you think you're not ready:

- Am I getting pleasure from my feelings of resentment and hate?

- Am I keeping an enemy so I can blame someone else for my misery?

- Does keeping a resentment make my life more exciting?

- Am I hanging on to my resentments to have an excuse to be violent, abusive, or angry?

- Am I clinging to my hate out of habit?

- Am I afraid to face a future without hate?

Forgiving is for you, not the person you forgive. Hate is a monkey on your back. It weighs you down. Hate may be destroying your life. Meanwhile, the person you hate may not know or care. He or she may even be dead.

Forgiving is a gift to yourself. You forgive so you can get on with your life.

Forgiving takes time. It's usually a slow process. You can't just snap your fingers and be done with it. But you can decide today it's something you want.

Forgiving means letting go of the past. The past can't change. It's over. Hate is a way of clinging to the past. But *forgiving doesn't mean forgetting,* either. You need to remember what happened so you can protect yourself.

You may have to forgive yourself. Sometimes you can't forgive others until you also forgive yourself. For all the hate you've been carrying around. For wasting years of your life resenting others. For stupid things you've done in the name of hate.

Ed decided to forgive. He did it for himself, not Lee. Sure, it took time, but it was worth it. Ed let go of the past. He quit going over and over what Lee did to him. But Ed did make a promise to be careful. He didn't want to have the same problems in his next romance. And, yes, Ed had to forgive himself. It helped when he realized that everybody gets their feet muddy when they walk through a swamp. Hate was his swamp. It took him a while to find his way out. But he made it. Will you?

Tips on Forgiving

Forgiving is a choice. You have to want it. You have to work for it. It doesn't just happen. Here are some things you can do to help you forgive.

- Make a list of the people you need to forgive. Do you need to include yourself?

- Write down the reasons you need to forgive them— how forgiving them will help you. How are your hatreds hurting you? What's happened to you because of your resentments?

- List the angry thoughts you have the most about each person.

- List the things you've done or are doing in the name of hate. Things like avoiding them, gossiping, putting sugar in their gas tank, making late night hang-up calls, and so on.

- Promise yourself to stop your hating thoughts and actions. Maybe you can't stop them all right away, but do what you can. You might have to start with one or two people on your list. That way you won't feel overwhelmed.

- Make another list. Write two or three good things about each person you resent ("Well, at least she's a good cook. And she did try to be there for us when she wasn't sick."). Forgiving means letting the other person be human again, not a monster. By the way, no "yeah, buts" allowed. Don't follow praise with criticism.

- Many people begin to forgive by praying for the person they hate. If that seems impossible, maybe you can think of one nice thing happening to them.

- If the person or people you hate are still in your life, you need to quit doing nasty stuff to them. At least get into neutral if you can't be decent. For instance, you don't have to walk out of a room just because they come in. You can sit there. You could even surprise everybody by being polite.

- Remember these phrases: "I will be patient with myself." "No strings attached." (This means you won't expect or demand anything from the people you forgive. You need to forgive without playing any games.) "Forgiving is for me, not them."

- Ask for help. Forgiving yourself can be hard. You might need help from friends, counselors, or the clergy.

Summary

Hate is the angry person's best dream and worst nightmare. Hate gives you a reason to stay angry, if that's what you want. But hate is a trap that you might never escape.

Forgiving is the way to let go of hate. Forgiving takes time, patience, and a real desire to change. You may have to forgive yourself as well as others. The goal is to heal old wounds so you can get on with your life.

10

I Need Help, Too— A Chapter for Partners of Angry People

Living with an angry person is hard work. It may be dangerous. It can even be fatal.

You won't get much praise or appreciation from the angry person. Instead, you get big complaints about little problems, endless criticism, and a lot of ridiculous tantrums.

But here you are, for better or worse. Somehow your spouse, partner, or friend is angry all the time. Maybe you didn't realize that at first. Perhaps you just figured it out.

You're in trouble. This isn't going to be easy. Living with a habitually angry person is like chewing on a lemon, hoping it will taste sweet. Chewing harder doesn't help. Adding sugar only covers up the sour taste for a while. And pretending a lemon is an orange won't do any good either.

You may have to spit that lemon out. But before you do, let's take a look at what you can do to make your life better. Here are my suggestions:

- Protect yourself. Physical safety comes first.

- Realize that you have the right to be treated with respect.

- Don't accept responsibility for your partner's anger.

- Watch your own anger. Don't become too angry yourself. But also don't become an anger avoider.

- Don't isolate. Get support from others.

- Think about what the angry person gains from his or her anger.

- Learn how you've been affected by your partner's anger.

- Think seriously about leaving if your partner won't or can't change.

Protect Yourself

Some angry people are violent. They hit, slap, bite, shove, and hold. They threaten. They are bullies who beat up anyone smaller or weaker. They're scary and dangerous.

You (and your children) have the right to be safe.

Nobody deserves to be hurt, no matter how angry the other person gets. I suppose you know that already. But do you believe it? For you?

The angry person is responsible for his or her actions. But if your partner is a batterer or child beater, you need a survival plan. You need to know what to do to protect yourself and your family.

I'm not saying you can make anybody else less mean or nasty. You can't. That's their job. And I'm not saying you can keep them from hitting or hurting you. You can't.

What you can do is protect yourself. You can draw up a plan of action that will help keep you a little safer some of the time. You might save your life by thinking ahead.

You may feel depressed and hopeless. That's normal if

you're living with someone who gets violent. He or she is trying to control you, to destroy your belief in yourself. Don't give in. You'll be stuck forever if you do, and you'll be miserable.

Sit down and make a plan. How can I stay safe? Where can I go? What can I do?

Is there a shelter you can go to in your community? A safe house? Do you know their phone numbers? Look them up. Memorize them!

Are there friends or family or neighbors you can go to? Think of the people close by you can count on.

Keep a few dollars on hand in case you have to get out fast. Leave at the first signs of trouble, before you are trapped. For instance, if your partner is out drinking, and you know he'll come home violent, don't wait around. Get out and get safe *now.*

What if flight is impossible? Maybe the rager is right in front of you, ready to strike. Try to stay calm. Use a steady voice. Walk and move slowly. Keep your distance if you can. Don't argue. Don't try to explain or justify your actions if that only gives the rageaholic more excuses to complain. Use quiet, unemotional language. Think of it as living through a bad storm by letting the wind pass right by. Your job is survival. Keep your mind on that task.

Calling the police may help. So can temporary restraining orders, but not always, and never if you break them yourself out of guilt or loneliness.

Nothing you say or do guarantees your safety. You're living with a violent person. But do what you can. Don't give up hope. And keep reading.

Realize That You Have the Right To Be Treated with Respect

I once saw a cartoon with two giraffes. The first looked normal. The second's back looked like a staircase. The second one asked the other: "I wonder why people keep stepping on me?"

I remember another cartoon. There's a man lying on the street. Cars are coming. The caption says something like this: "Having low self-esteem, George takes a job as a speed bump."

You've got to believe in yourself. That you are a good person. That you are worthwhile. Above all, that you deserve respect*.

Being treated with respect means no name-calling, yelling, swearing, put-downs, or criticism. No hitting, punching, slapping. No holding. No threats.

It means being listened to and taken seriously. Without interruptions. With the TV turned off. It means you can state your feelings without apology.

You have a right to your own thoughts. You have the right to say yes or no about things that affect your life.

You have the right to be human and make mistakes, without paying forever for them. You don't have to be perfect to be lovable.

You have a life of your own. Your partner is part of that life but not all of it. You can have your own friends, hobbies, and career. *You haven't been put on this planet just to take care of others*, including the angry or violent person.

Above all, you have the right to be whoever you are. You have the right to feel worthwhile and valued. To do things your way. To be respected, not owned.

Don't expect your partner to remind you of these rights. Nobody gives up power willingly. Begin by treating yourself and others with respect. Then seek it from your partner. Expect a lot of resistance. You'll be told you're selfish. You'll feel guilty even when you've done nothing bad, just because you're not spending all your time being nice to someone who isn't nice to you. But don't give up. Remember, unless you do something, you may live unhappily the rest of your life.

---

* See *I Deserve Respect*, by Ron and Pat Potter-Efron (Center City, MN: Hazelden Press, 1989). Also, some of this material is from Pat Potter-Efron's "Partner's Bill of Rights," published in Ron and Pat Potter-Efron's *Anger, Alcoholism, and Addiction* (New York: W.W. Norton, 1992).

Don't Accept Responsibility for Your Partner's Anger

You aren't the cause of your partner's anger. You aren't the solution.

You aren't the cause. Some people are severely angry. They've been that way a long time. Probably from long before you even met. If they weren't angry at you, they would be angry at somebody else.

The anger problem belongs to the angry person. He or she is the only one who can do anything about it.

Of course angry people blame others. They always say "You make me mad." But that isn't the truth. They make themselves mad. They're just trying to give away responsibility for their own behavior. That's one of the main ways angry people stay angry (see Chapter 3 for the other ways). If they blame others for making them mad, then they can be an innocent victim.

That's bull.

We each must take responsibility for our own actions. Me for mine. You for yours. Your partner for his or hers. The same is true for anger. Mine is mine. Yours is yours. I'm not the cause of yours. You're not the cause of mine.

You aren't the solution. That means you can't fix your angry partner. Not by being sweet. Not by being mean. Not even by being assertive.

Have you noticed there is a serious shortage of magic wands in this universe? Maybe you should give up looking for one that would turn your frog into a prince or princess. You need to focus your energy on yourself, not your partner. Figure out who you are. Take time with yourself instead of always thinking about him or her. Detach.

Maybe you've been trying for years to fix your partner. So he or she will be nicer to you. Or calm down. Or quit harping about little things. You've thought and thought. You've argued, maneuvered, pleaded, and reasoned. How well has it worked?

Probably not very well. Because your partner has to see the problem and want to change. Until then, all your effort is wasted.

I'm not saying you should stop fighting for what you want. Just don't kid yourself. You have very limited power here. You can make suggestions, but you can't cure your partner.

To repeat: You aren't the cause of your partner's anger. You aren't the solution.

Watch Your Own Anger

Remember *Goldilocks and the Three Bears*? Goldilocks liked the middle-sized chair. She preferred porridge that was neither too hot nor too cold. She avoided extremes.

Avoiding extremes—especially with your own anger—is important when you live with an angry person. You can easily get too hot. Then you become another angry person. You lose your temper more often. When you do get angry, you're louder, meaner, and nastier than ever before. You may get violent, too. And it's harder to let go of your resentments, so you stay on the edge of anger all the time. Finally, you lash out at more and more people, even the ones you try to protect from your partner's anger.

This is no good. You're fast developing your own anger problem. Sure, you can blame your partner. But that's just an excuse. It won't help you stop. You need to make and keep a promise to quit destroying your life with your anger.

It's easy to get too cold. Then you try to avoid all your anger. You do that partly out of fear ("If I'm really nice and never get angry he won't get mad at me as often."). Or to set an example ("I want the kids to see that you don't ever have to be angry."). Maybe it's how you grew up ("We never raised our voices. Mom and Dad never fought."). Or to feel superior ("I refuse to be childish like him. I'm better than that.").

The more your partner rages, the more you deny your anger. I know this is partly a matter of survival. There are many times when the only thing to do is to keep quiet. But the cost to you is great. You're becoming an anger avoider.

You deny your own anger, even when it's justified. Remember that anger itself is a God-given feeling. It tells you something is wrong. Anger pushes you to act. You'll never get the message if you won't listen to the messenger.

So be like Goldilocks. Keep your relationship with anger normal. Find a middle ground where you have some anger but not too much.

Here are few ideas that will help you keep your anger at a normal level:

- You don't have to get angry every time your partner gets angry.

- You don't have to give in or be nice every time your partner gets angry.

- Don't deflect your anger at your partner onto others. Getting angry at your kids, for instance, won't help when you're actually mad at your partner.

- Be assertive. That means clearly telling people what you want and need, without blaming or attacking. (There are many books and classes on assertiveness; a good book is *Your Perfect Right*.*)

- Above all, take responsibility for your own anger and your own life. If you have an anger problem (too much or too little), do something about it now.

Get Support from Others

I have a saying: *Someone can't be both the problem and the solution at the same time.* Your partner's behavior is the problem. So don't expect him or her to be the one who can comfort you. Or understand you. Or immediately change their actions. You're in big trouble if your partner is the only person you can turn to about the problem.

---

* *Your Perfect Right, Second Edition,* by Robert Alberti and Michael Emmons, published in 1990 by Impact Press, San Luis Obispo, CA.

Besides, the angry person gains power and control when she cuts you off from others. If all you hear is her voice, pretty soon you will think like she does. You'll end up blaming yourself for "making her mad." Your mind gets confused, your ideas distorted. But there's nobody around to help you think better.

Get help! Friends, family, ministers, and counselors may be part of the picture. Therapy and self-help groups are really useful. They give you a bunch of fellow travelers with whom you can share experiences. There's nothing like hearing, "Sure, that's what she said to me, too. But it was all a pack of lies. Don't believe everything they say." You would listen politely if a counselor told you that. But the words have more impact when they come from another person who lives or lived with someone who was angry all the time.

You lose track of "normal" when your partner is so angry. You need people who can remind you what normal is.

Plus, this is tough work. It's hard to change your life anytime, especially now. You can get very discouraged. You may feel like giving up. You may have suicidal thoughts. You need a support system to help you through the bad times.

Sometimes partners of angry people ask for help only when there is an immediate problem. That won't work. It's like only watering your garden during a drought. Gardens need tending even on good days. So do you. You need people in your life. Normal people.

Maybe you need to put this book down and make a call right now.

What Does Your Partner Gain?

Your recovery is mostly about you, not your partner. Still, it's good to know all you can about why the rager rages. It may help you stay safe. It may let you quit playing useless mind games. So study the situation but don't dwell on it. Try to be objective. Focus on facts and patterns.

Please read or review Chapters 2 and 3, where I talk about how very angry people become and stay angry.

Most excessively angry people want power and control. They get angry to get what they want. The more that works, the angrier they get. If your partner's anger is mostly about power and control, you'll have to show him it won't work. It's important not to give in to a bully. He needs to learn you won't be bullied into doing what he wants.

You don't have to get angry back, however. That's playing into the game. A calm but firm no is usually better. Expect to be tested, though. He may get angrier before he calms down. But stand your ground, unless it's physically dangerous. In that case you need to get safe first. Don't give in to a power play.

I can offer two ideas that might help if power or control is the issue. First, some partners try to ignore the angry person. This works best when you've clearly told the person before that you won't talk when he or she is yelling or blaming. Once they calm down it is important to talk with them.

Another useful idea is to talk only about the facts of a situation. In this case you speak with them, but you don't even comment if they start to make personal attacks. For instance, your partner is angry because you bought new shoes. You discuss the matter as long as she sticks to the budget. But you ignore any extra insults (such as "you're always so irresponsible"). If that doesn't work, you inform her that you will talk about the topic only as long as she doesn't shame or blame. If she keeps going, refuse to continue.

People rage for many other reasons: excitement/intensity, to keep people away, to hide other feelings, to defend against low self-worth, as part of alcoholism or drug addiction. Your choices about what to do will be different with each reason. Learn what you can about what it is your partner gains from his or her anger.

People who seek intensity want you to join in the game of excited misery. Instead, you'll want to stay calm. It's not nearly as much fun to play that game alone. They'll often quit after a while.

The man or woman who gets angry to keep you away is afraid of emotional closeness. You alone can't change that, but you can help by keeping your distance or approaching slowly. Your partner needs to deal with that fear of closeness, perhaps in therapy.

Maybe the rager is hiding other feelings. If so, a simple "What else are you feeling right now?" could help. But don't try this without discussing it with your partner first. And don't assume that their rage always is just a cover for other feelings.

Many angry people feel awful about themselves. Their rage against others is part of their own self-hatred. That's not an excuse for their actions, though. They need to start doing something to begin liking themselves more.

What if the problem involves low self-esteem? Your partner might rage a lot when he or she feels ashamed, inadequate, or not good enough. Well, that's sad, but *the answer to their self-esteem problem isn't to crush or destroy yours.* Of course, the angry person thinks, "If I can make you feel awful, then I'll feel better." That's like one broken egg cracking another in order to feel whole. It won't work. But it sure makes a mess. You may both need help if this has been going on a long time. It's important for you to talk to people who like and respect you. Get away from the criticism, at least once in a while. It will help you stay sane.

Don't drink or use drugs with your partner. Discourage (without lecturing) the use of mood-altering substances. Be careful about your own use, too. It's easy to cover up your pain with booze when your partner is angry all the time.

Learn. Think. Experiment. But remember, you alone can't change your partner. Your job is to change yourself. To get off your partner's roller coaster. To get a life of your own.

How Are You Affected?

This is about "before and after." What were you like *before* you got involved with this angry person? What are you like *now*?

How have your *feelings* changed? Are you scared more now? Are you more angry? Do you stuff your feelings when you used to talk about them? Do you feel lonelier? Happier? More or less alive? Depressed? Suicidal?

What about your *thoughts*? Have you become confused? Unable to think straight? Does it seem like you're going crazy? Do you spend most of your time worrying about your partner? Are you thinking your own thoughts, or have you taken in your partner's? Can you even tell the difference? Or have you decided not to think about anything at all anymore?

Now take a look at your *actions*. What do you do to keep the rager from raging? What have you quit doing out of fear or to keep the peace? Can you do what you want, when you want, the way you want? Or is everything up to him or her? Do you feel free? Do you feel trapped?

How has your *self-concept* been affected? How do you feel about yourself? Are you a good person? If 0 equals no self-worth and 100 equals great self-worth, where are you today? Where were you before? What happened?

Have there been any changes in your *religious or spiritual beliefs or behaviors*? Have you lost faith? Have you changed churches (if so, was it something you really wanted to do)? Does the rager have strange or extreme religious beliefs you are expected to follow? Do you feel connected with the universe, or disconnected, cut off from everything but your partner?

What about *long-term gains and losses* as a result of being the partner of an angry person? Use the checklist on the following page to measure gains or losses in important areas of your life.

Ask yourself these questions:

- Overall, are you better or worse off?

- What do you need to do to improve your life in these areas?

- What can you do with the help of your partner?

- What must you do despite him or her?

What if Your Partner Won't or Can't Change?

Life is hard when you have to choose between staying in a bad relationship and facing the unknown alone.

Area	Gains	Losses
Hope		
Love		
Health		
Money		
Work		
Family		
Friends		
Safety		
Pride		
Peace of mind		
Sanity		
Self		

Leaving is the last step.

First, do all you can to improve yourself. That includes taking a good look at your own words and deeds. Do what you need to do so you're part of the solution, not part of the problem. Look at your own anger. Do your share to drain the tension from the relationship.

Next, insist upon change. You have the right to tell your partner you won't live this way anymore. It's bad for you and hard on the kids. You don't plan to live the rest of your life worried, anxious, and afraid.

Warning: Don't tell your partner you're going to leave immediately, unless you are prepared to do so. It's better to say that you won't hang around forever; sooner or later you're leaving unless he or she does something to change.

Be as clear as you can.

> George, here's what has to change. You've got to stop calling me ugly and stupid. No more threats to hit me, either, or to take away the kids. And I need you to listen to me when I speak with you. That means us spending time together with the television off.

Or

> Sandra, the yelling has to stop. The jealous accusations. And I insist you see a doctor or therapist to check on your depression. I think that may be why you've gotten so angry.

Don't accept vague promises from your partner. It's a good start if she says she'll go to counseling. But it's only the beginning. Let's see if she follows through. As for George's apology for name-calling, that's great. But you've heard that before. This time he better start making an honest effort to treat you with respect.

Many angry people can and do change. That's what most of this book is for. Life can get better for both of you.

Some won't or can't change. If so, you might have to leave to have a decent life.

Give them a chance. Give them a dozen chances. But you've got to face reality. If they don't change, the relationship will stay bad. Their anger will seep into your soul. You'll be unhappy. You'll stay unhappy.

Your partner must take responsibility for his or her anger. It's not your fault when they don't.

Everybody has a right to live a good life. Even you. I hope, for both of you, that turns out to be with your partner. But do what you must. You, too, are responsible for your fate.

Summary

Living with an angry person can be awful. We've looked at some things you can do to face the situation, though. If you do stay in it, you'll need to fight hard to get treated decently. Your safety comes first, of course. Then the right to be treated with respect. If all else fails, you may have to get out.

Try to be both realistic and hopeful. If you can't be both, be realistic. Your health and sanity depend upon it.

11

Where Do I Go from Here?

If you're still with me, you may have already taken some action to control your anger. Maybe you've made yourself a promise to stay calm for at least twenty-four hours. Or you've taken steps to climb down the anger and violence ladder. You've at least done a lot of thinking about where your anger came from and where it's headed. So, where do you go from here?

This chapter helps you to ask for what you want without threatening. It shows you how to fight fair—to handle disagreements without going back to your old angry ways. It finishes up with a quick review and a suggestion.

Asking for What You Want

My friend Charlie Rumberg runs a program for batterers. He's told me about a pattern he sees in his clients. (I've changed a few things here, but the basic idea is Charlie's.)

- First they *ask* for what they want. But if they don't get it, then . . .

- they try to *persuade* the other. But if that doesn't work, then . . .

- they get *sneaky*, manipulating, and cunning. If that fails, then . . .

- they *threaten* to hurt the other in some way ("do it or else"). And if they still don't get what they want, then . . .

- they *attack*.

Here's an example. Shirley wants to go out tonight with her boyfriend Bill. She asks, but Bill has other plans. He has a test the next day he has to study for.

Shirley tries persuasion next. "Oh, come on, you know you'll have a great time. You can always study tomorrow." But no, Bill really has to study.

OK, time for sneaky maneuvers. How about a guilt trip? "Bill, you owe it to me. Remember, I went out with you last week when I had a test the next day. Come on." Whine, whimper, cry. Who cares about Bill's needs? I want to go out, now.

That didn't do it, either. Better threaten. "Look, Bill, I said we're going out tonight and I mean it. I can go out with some other guy if you won't take me." Bill says again that he just can't take her out. This is the biggest test of the whole term. He has to do well to stay in school.

Totally frustrated, Shirley smacks Bill on his chest, breaks into tears of rage, and runs out of the room. If she were a little bigger, she'd try to drag him out of his room.

What a waste. That's not my idea of how to ask for what you want. Here's a better way.

Don't make an ass of yourself. That's the bottom line. Asking for what you want means just that—asking. No more whining, pleading, demanding, threatening, guilt-tripping, repeating, lying, and bull-shitting.

Don't confuse wants with needs. A *need* is something you can't survive without: bread, water, air. A *want* makes life better: a new car, sex, a good job. You don't like it, but you survive if you don't get what you want.

Ninety-nine percent of what we ask for are wants. So don't act like you're going to die if you don't get some of them. Don't explode just because your partner made spaghetti instead of steak. Be grateful you have spaghetti. Be glad you've got a partner. You want steak but you don't need it.

Tell others what you want. Be direct, specific, and polite. This is just like the tenth rule in Chapter 7. That's where you tell others exactly what's bothering you. Here you tell them exactly what you want.

Be direct. That means don't hint around. Don't hope they'll figure it out, then get mad and feel hurt if they don't. "Tonight I'd like to go to the movies, Hon."

Be specific. Whatever you leave out now may be the start of a fight later. So let the other person know exactly what you want. "I mean, I want to see *Schindler's List*, not just any movie."

Be polite. There is no need for threats and guilt trips. Remember, this is a want, not a need.

Give the real reason you want what you want. I know, it's a lousy con. But sometimes the truth actually works. And it leads to fewer fights than lies and half-truths. "To be honest, I'm tired of mystery shows. And I've heard *Schindler's List* is a movie that makes you think."

Be willing to negotiate and compromise. You can't always get just what you want when you want it. Sometimes you have to talk things over. You don't always have to give in, though. Good partnerships usually are fifty-fifty deals. "OK, you really don't want to see *Schindler's List* tonight. But you'll go with me tomorrow. Fine. What do you want to do tonight?"

It's not really all that hard. But you need to practice asking for what you want. Start now and keep going. You won't always get what you want, of course. But you'll do well enough, and you'll avoid useless arguments.

Fair Fighting

Let's discuss one last problem. No two people agree on everything. That means some conflict is normal. But how can you handle disagreements without going back to your old angry ways?

Below is a list of fair fighting rules. Follow them and you'll stay out of trouble.

Fair Fighting Rules

Do	Don't
tell people what you feel	make fun of others
stick to one issue at a time	hit, push, shove, hold, or threaten to do so
sit down and talk	
listen	stand up and yell
focus on the specific behavior you want	make faces
	attack the other's personality
make regular eye contact (but don't glare)	name-call
be flexible—be willing to change your mind	get stuck in the past
	run away from the issue
breathe calmly, stay relaxed	say "forget it," "tough," "I don't care," "so what," or anything that ignores the other's concerns
be open to negotiation and compromise	
be responsible for everything you say	
	have to get the last word in
focus on solutions, not victories or defeats	interrupt
take time-outs as needed	say "always" or "never" or other generalizations

---

Take a good look at these do's and don'ts. Circle the items on the don'ts list that are hardest for you. Circle the do that you most need to follow. Then practice, practice, practice.

If you lose your temper, go back to this list. You'll almost certainly find you broke a few don'ts, or you forgot a few do's.

You need to do four things when you make an anger mistake. First, admit it to yourself. Second, admit it to others. Third, apologize and do what you can to undo the damage. Fourth, commit to changing that behavior so you don't make the same mistake again.

Finishing Up

We've covered a lot of ground in this book. By now, you have

- Recognized you are a person with a big anger problem
- Looked at how your anger has affected yourself and others
- Thought about how you became so angry
- Considered the main reasons you've stayed angry
- Made a sincere promise to yourself to change
- Walked up and down the anger and violence ladder
- Studied eleven rules to be less angry and violent
- Read about the problems of paranoia and resentment

I hope you've also taken a peek at the chapter written for your partner. If so, you saw that he or she has a lot of things to think about.

What now? I'd suggest rereading this book, slowly. This time concentrate on the practical suggestions. Figure out what you need to do most to get yourself started on a new life. Plan on working hard, making a few mistakes, and learning from them.

Don't just *try* to do better, though. Trying is dying. You've got to get past trying into doing. Remember, this is your chance to live a normal life. Don't blow it.

Let's review the eleven important rules for controlling your anger once more:

1. Take a time-out to stop the violence.

2. Wipe that frown off your face and relax.

3. Quit trying to control others.

4. Accept difference.

5. Ask, don't demand.

6. Reward, don't punish or threaten.

7. Speak quietly and don't swear.

8. Be responsible for what you say.

9. Treat others with respect.

10. Tell others what bothers you. Be direct, specific, and polite.

11. Use "I" statements.

You can have a normal life—one free from rage, violence, resentment, and useless anger. It's your choice.

Some Other New Harbinger Self-Help Titles

Scarred Soul, $13.95
The Angry Heart, $13.95
Don't Take It Personally, $12.95
Becoming a Wise Parent For Your Grown Child, $12.95
Clear Your Past, Change Your Future, $12.95
Preparing for Surgery, $17.95
Coming Out Everyday, $13.95
Ten Things Every Parent Needs to Know, $12.95
The Power of Two, $12.95
It's Not OK Anymore, $13.95
The Daily Relaxer, $12.95
The Body Image Workbook, $17.95
Living with ADD, $17.95
Taking the Anxiety Out of Taking Tests, $12.95
The Taking Charge of Menopause Workbook, $17.95
Living with Angina, $12.95
PMS: Women Tell Women How to Control Premenstrual Syndrome, $13.95
Five Weeks to Healing Stress: The Wellness Option, $17.95
Choosing to Live: How to Defeat Suicide Through Cognitive Therapy, $12.95
Why Children Misbehave and What to Do About It, $14.95
Illuminating the Heart, $13.95
When Anger Hurts Your Kids, $12.95
The Addiction Workbook, $17.95
The Mother's Survival Guide to Recovery, $12.95
The Chronic Pain Control Workbook, Second Edition, $17.95
Fibromyalgia & Chronic Myofascial Pain Syndrome, $19.95
Diagnosis and Treatment of Sociopaths, $44.95
Flying Without Fear, $12.95
Kid Cooperation: How to Stop Yelling, Nagging & Pleading and Get Kids to Cooperate, $12.95
The Stop Smoking Workbook: Your Guide to Healthy Quitting, $17.95
Conquering Carpal Tunnel Syndrome and Other Repetitive Strain Injuries, $17.95
The Tao of Conversation, $12.95
Wellness at Work: Building Resilience for Job Stress, $17.95
What Your Doctor Can't Tell You About Cosmetic Surgery, $13.95
An End to Panic: Breakthrough Techniques for Overcoming Panic Disorder, $17.95
Living Without Procrastination: How to Stop Postponing Your Life, $12.95
Goodbye Mother, Hello Woman: Reweaving the Daughter Mother Relationship, $14.95
Letting Go of Anger: The 10 Most Common Anger Styles and What to Do About Them, $12.95
Messages: The Communication Skills Workbook, Second Edition, $13.95
Coping With Chronic Fatigue Syndrome: Nine Things You Can Do, $12.95
The Anxiety & Phobia Workbook, Second Edition, $17.95
Thueson's Guide to Over-the-Counter Drugs, $13.95
Natural Women's Health: A Guide to Healthy Living for Women of Any Age, $13.95
I'd Rather Be Married: Finding Your Future Spouse, $13.95
The Relaxation & Stress Reduction Workbook, Fourth Edition, $17.95
Living Without Depression & Manic Depression: A Workbook for Maintaining Mood Stability, $17.95
Coping With Schizophrenia: A Guide For Families, $13.95
Visualization for Change, Second Edition, $13.95
Postpartum Survival Guide, $13.95
Angry All the Time: An Emergency Guide to Anger Control, $12.95
Couple Skills: Making Your Relationship Work, $13.95
Stepfamily Realities: How to Overcome Difficulties and Have a Happy Family, $13.95
The Chemotherapy Survival Guide, $11.95
The Deadly Diet, Second Edition: Recovering from Anorexia & Bulimia, $13.95
Last Touch: Preparing for a Parent's Death, $11.95
Self-Esteem, Second Edition, $13.95
I Can't Get Over It, A Handbook for Trauma Survivors, Second Edition, $15.95
Dying of Embarrassment: Help for Social Anxiety and Social Phobia, $12.95
The Depression Workbook: Living With Depression and Manic Depression, $17.95
Prisoners of Belief: Exposing & Changing Beliefs that Control Your Life, $12.95
Men & Grief: A Guide for Men Surviving the Death of a Loved One, $13.95
When the Bough Breaks: A Helping Guide for Parents of Sexually Abused Children, $11.95
When Once Is Not Enough: Help for Obsessive Compulsives, $13.95
The Three Minute Meditator, Third Edition, $12.95
Beyond Grief: A Guide for Recovering from the Death of a Loved One, $13.95
Leader's Guide to the Relaxation & Stress Reduction Workbook, Fourth Edition, $19.95
The Divorce Book, $13.95
Hypnosis for Change: A Manual of Proven Techniques, Third Edition, $13.95
When Anger Hurts, $13.95
Lifetime Weight Control, $12.95

Call **toll free, 1-800-748-6273,** to order. Have your Visa or Mastercard number ready. Or send a check for the titles you want to New Harbinger Publications, Inc., 5674 Shattuck Ave., Oakland, CA 94609. Include $3.80 for the first book and 75¢ for each additional book, to cover shipping and handling. (California residents please include appropriate sales tax.) Allow four to six weeks for delivery.

Prices subject to change without notice.